Moon Pix

Pra

It was only a matter of time
is an audience for whom *E*
significant and worthy of study

The series … is freewheeling and eclectic, ranging from minute rock-geek analysis to idiosyncratic personal celebration—*The New York Times Book Review*

Ideal for the rock geek who thinks liner notes just aren't enough—*Rolling Stone*

One of the coolest publishing imprints on the planet—*Bookslut*

These are for the insane collectors out there who appreciate fantastic design, well-executed thinking, and things that make your house look cool. Each volume in this series takes a seminal album and breaks it down in startling minutiae. We love these. We are huge nerds—*Vice*

A brilliant series … each one a work of real love—*NME* (UK)

Passionate, obsessive, and smart—*Nylon*

Religious tracts for the rock 'n' roll faithful—*Boldtype*

[A] consistently excellent series—*Uncut* (UK)

We … aren't naive enough to think that we're your only source for reading about music (but if we had our way … watch out). For those of you who really like to know everything there is to know about an album, you'd do well to check out Bloomsbury's "33 1/3" series of books—*Pitchfork*

For reviews of individual titles in the series, please visit our blog at 333sound.com

and our website at http://www.bloomsbury.com/musicandsoundstudies

Follow us on Twitter: @333books

Like us on Facebook: https://www.facebook.com/33.3books

For a complete list of books in this series, see the back of this book.

Forthcoming in the series:

and many more …

Moon Pix

Donna Kozloskie

BLOOMSBURY ACADEMIC
NEW YORK • LONDON • OXFORD • NEW DELHI • SYDNEY

BLOOMSBURY ACADEMIC
Bloomsbury Publishing Inc
1385 Broadway, New York, NY 10018, USA
50 Bedford Square, London, WC1B 3DP, UK
29 Earlsfort Terrace, Dublin 2, Ireland

BLOOMSBURY, BLOOMSBURY ACADEMIC and the Diana logo are trademarks of
Bloomsbury Publishing Plc

First published in the United States of America 2022

Copyright © Donna Kozloskie, 2022

Library of Congress Cataloging-in-Publication Data
Names: Kozloskie, Donna, author.
Title: Moon Pix / Donna Kozloskie.
Description: [1st.] | New York : Bloomsbury Academic, 2022. |
Series: 33 1/3 | Includes bibliographical references. |
Summary: "Moon Pix was conceived during a hallucinatory waking nightmare in
the South Carolina home of Chan Marshall one fateful day in 1997. Like all legends,
the aura surrounding them is an impression, a sensory feeling of unreliable
memories: layers of stories become histories. Through interviews with key players,
audience member accounts, fictional narrative imaginings, a collection of record
reviews and other explorations of truth, this book, like Moon Pix itself, is an ode to
the myth within the music and the music within the myth"– Provided by publisher.
Identifiers: LCCN 2021052888 (print) | LCCN 2021052889 (ebook) |
ISBN 9781501377938 (paperback) | ISBN 9781501377945 (epub) |
ISBN 9781501377952 (pdf) | ISBN 9781501377969
Subjects: LCSH: Cat Power, 1972-. Moon pix. | Cat Power,
1972—Criticism and interpretation.
Classification: LCC ML420.C35 K69 2022 (print) | LCC ML420.C35 (ebook) |
DDC 782.42164092–dc23
LC record available at https://lccn.loc.gov/2021052888
LC ebook record available at https://lccn.loc.gov/2021052889

ISBN: PB: 978-1-5013-7793-8
            ePDF: 978-1-5013-7795-2
            eBook: 978-1-5013-7794-5

Series: 33 1/3

Typeset by Integra Software Services Pvt. Ltd.
Printed and bound in the United States of America

To find out more about our authors and books visit
www.bloomsbury.com and sign up for our newsletters.

Contents

CONTENTS

Author's Note

Hello, nice to meet you!

This book is a refraction of *Moon Pix*.

It's a shattering of each track into the pieces that bring it to life and thoughts about your place in that shattering and life—yes, you!

And it's not boring!

Welcome to this book.

(gently drops needle on opening track: "*My friend ….*")

1

American Flag

In 1996, "The World's Only Klan Museum" opened its doors in South Carolina—defiantly, brazenly, announcing itself on a marquee in downtown Laurens to mixed reviews. The fact that the reviews were mixed says a lot. The fact that the space once operated as The Echo Theater, a segregated movie house, also says a lot.

A year later, about an hour east, in a South Carolina farmhouse in Prosperity (a town with an average population of 1,000), Chan Marshall sat awake for days. Her boyfriend was away for work, and the domestic life she dreamed of was beginning to lose its wonder. She was in bed with her kitten (possibly named Blackie Brown Blanco Jerry Seinfeld), while her Bible and a copy of Denis Johnson's *Already Dead* sat on her nightstand. She was alone in a white suburban-looking house with aluminum awnings for one, two, or three months. Beyond the fields that stretched behind the property were the highway and train tracks, ways out toward what passed for towns. A used car dealership sat still, broken tractor parts settled into the ground. Crickets and darkness filled the empty spaces. Chan heard the sound of something out in the fields.

The ground began to shake deeply. She felt a presence, like a tornado had sieged on her quiet, empty home. A rattling, booming voice spoke, "Chan, come and meet me outside, and all the past will be forgotten." She began to pray. She shouted: "No, I won't meet you!" She ran from room to room, turning on lights, moving from window to window, looking for the source of the otherworldly words. She could feel an energy, she saw spirits coiling around the window panes of her tired mind. A giant mass of souls rolled against the house like a wave, their see-through gray bodies trying to force their way into reality. They roiled in the blackness of the night given shape as they swirled, pushing in on her heaving windows, threatening through the trees, pressuring her to action—to move or be moved—by whatever this was. "No. No." she asserted, their bulging chants pushed away with each defiant "no." Turning on the lights made them recede, their undulating mass evaporating with each flicked switch. Chan would not let them in.

At that moment, she sat on her bed and realized how fragile her life was. If people were to find her body in the aftermath of whatever this nightmare was, she wanted to leave behind evidence of her fate. She grabbed her acoustic guitar, and into a tape recorder, she sang. She sang what would become most of the album *Moon Pix*.

The next morning, still trying to externalize her waking nightmare, she drove eleven hours straight to New York City. While there, she tried explaining to her friends what had happened. She wanted to convey her terrifying moment of panic. She was looking for understanding. Her words washed over their jaded city demeanors, a few worried about her, but there was no action. How do you tell a story to make people listen? How do you get others to experience your experience? Unable to communicate, she drove back to South Carolina.

Two days later (or maybe the same day or maybe even before her vision, depending on what account you believe), still rattled by the experience, a friend phoned. He wanted to shake some sense into her. To tell her she needed to bring her music into the universe. He was convinced she was wasting her life, hiding out in a domestic dream, trying to get away from music. He knew what was best. Her phone rang again. She picked it up to learn one of her friends had died. Later that night, another close friend passed away; one of the friends was her first drummer. The news awakened Chan. Again, she realized she needed to act. She went to a fax machine somewhere. She reached out to Jim White and Mick Turner of the Australian trio Dirty Three, whom she had previously toured alongside. She called her label, Matador, and was given money to travel to Melbourne to work on a new album.

Before settling into music, she spent three months traveling to New Zealand, Tasmania, and Australia. She traveled to the West Coast of Australia, where she graced the clear watered beaches and limestone caverns of Yallingup. She stayed afloat in a saltwater lake. She swam in a body of water abutting tea trees, their roots steeping the water with tinted, healing oils, emerging to dry in the warmth of Summer. She floated in a saltwater tub while listening to the meditations of an orange-clad sex cult. She traveled to the Eastcoast of Byron Bay. She made friends at a hostel. Together they dove off of cliffs and swam with sharks. They would boogie board every day. In Northern Queensland, near Brisbane, green mountains towered along the sandy beach. She rode big horses along the shoreline with a gallop, grabbing onto the neck of a wild companion who crashed into the waves with speed. She drank beer and BBQed, joined at times by Jim and Mick and, on one occasion, Will Oldham, a fellow traveling musician from the US South, baking together in a different hemisphere. Chan soaked up the autonomy. She reveled in the change of scenery; her farmhouse nightmare was a distant memory.

Chan played around with music in Jim White's house in Melbourne. Jim's talent, subtle winks of acknowledgment, and frank honesty make one feel comfortable with whatever vision they might have, no matter how daunting or singular; he forces people to trust their instincts. The acoustics of Jim's bathroom were perfect for recording demos, a single microphone swallowing up the loose guitar, shaky yet forthright vocals, and surreal lyrics. "Peking Saint" and "You May Know Him" were recorded in Mick's bedroom (a.k.a. Scuzz Studios). At the end of December, Jim prodded about studio time, mentioning that Mick was to travel and if they wanted to record, they needed to do so soon. Chan tried to book a session for New Years Day; the engineer at Sing Sing Studios in Melbourne said no. Recording began on the 2nd of January, 1998.

Sing Sing was built by Kaj Dahlstrom, a Swedish musician who moved into the recording realm in the mid-70s and founded the studio in the Richmond area of Melbourne. A brick fortress on the outside, the interior is the opposite, with soft, natural lighting, plants seeping into the space. Dahlstrom's woodworking spreads throughout, taking on the form of precise cabinets, abstract sculptures, gleaming floors. Muted tones of greens and yellows give a subtle glow, Persian rugs blanket floors and walls while welcoming, overstuffed couches feel like home. A kitchen with white wooden cabinets, red countertops, and exposed brick adds another familiar embrace. Vintage microphones, Neve recording consoles, and grand pianos are tucked into nooks waiting to be brought to life.

Chan appeared alone in the studio, a rap CD in her bag. With a clear aural vision, she asked for a song to be played in reverse. The sample became the base of *Moon Pix*'s first track, "American Flag," which took a whole day to record. Chan seemed to have mostly spent time recording in the background, possibly a mix of classic industry misogyny and the slight naivete, or fear, felt in youth (she would turn twenty-six at the end of the month). This session marked one of the first times she asked for what she wanted musically, and she got it. No person was standing between her and the sound, no one lecturing on how to respect the music or someone with much more experience forging a path. This sample was a turning point, the perfect introduction to the album and Chan's familiar yet mildly warped aesthetic that would define Cat Power.

Chan sang her songs while playing the guitar, unearthing the emotions embedded within them. At times she would fall into tears, crumpled into submission by herself. The engineer, Matt Voigt, reassured that it was all working; there was no need to weep. Her life clawed itself out across the songs, replaying relationships and memories—some good, some bad—as almost all the songs on *Moon Pix* seem rooted in a real sense of something or someone, even if written in a jarring hallucination.

A few days later, Jim and Mick came to the studio for a quick session. They mostly played over the pre-recorded tracks from the previous days. Jim was kept rhythmically engaged, each of his limbs dicing beats into milliseconds as usual but made even more challenging by the lack of metronome on the tracks. A flutist came in to add an eerie flutter, and a bassist on double bass arrived too. "Colors and the Kids" was written and recorded in the studio with the vocal and piano recorded simultaneously. The cover of "Moonshiner" was inspired by Bob Dylan's version, this one with Chan's lyrical turns and emotive sedation. Two other songs didn't make it to the album. One was a cover Chan had been playing for years by her old friend from Atlanta, Debbie Richardson, who had a band called Magic Bone. Another track was written in her South Carolina dream called "Staleyyawn" (said to be the name of a horse). This nearly eight-minute track, later renamed "When on the Mountaintops" or "Mountaintops," appeared on an album of rarities, its tone almost triumphant, full of acceptance.

Throughout the process of recording, Matt and Chan would try to figure each other out while Jim would sit on a couch reading from whatever was lying around, like sugary music gossip magazines. If Jim sensed Chan needed support, he would emerge from behind whatever he was reading, reinforce her wishes, and return to reading about people like Courtney Love. When the engineer asked about the origin of her songs, Chan mentioned a trip to Mexico as her inspiration. Another time, she credited a trip to South Africa. She also spoke of the songs coming to her a night that she thought she was going to die. She blurred her visions in a multitude of truths. Her tales were myths, and myths make legends. *Moon Pix* was destined for legend, as was her tour for the album.

Some came for the music, others for the show, and the show sometimes consisted of Chan leaving or hiding behind a piano or an amp. One account said that when she emerged from behind her hiding place, her pants were unbuttoned. It has been said she mooned an audience and threatened another to sue her. At one eventful show, she came into the audience and lay facedown on the floor as fans patted her back. Other common gestures included berating herself on stage or apologizing profusely for each move. Not every performance was like this, though. Some shows were sublime. Chan would dip in and out of the microphone with precision, creating a distancing, supernatural sonic space that audiences would float inside of. The whole room would go still with quiet reverence. But good shows are rarely the ones that live on. Conflict is so much easier to convey than the transcendent.

Even though she wasn't waitressing anymore, touring seemed like a different kind of serving, a more taxing, spiritual one. It's hard to explain the feeling of an indie rock tour; it's a singular physical sensation, one of dislocation—a constant in-between existence. It's a mix of dehydration, stale air, exhaustion, and wonder. One is moving from place to place, seeing new things, meeting new people with joy but also with little sleep. By the time one starts to absorb a place in any meaningful way, they are piling back into a vehicle with the same group of people, hurtling toward the next target on the map, and hoping that those in the room next door will go to bed at a reasonable time. Band members also meet up with people they know that are scattered throughout the route, small detours or drinks that suddenly plunge one into their past. This bone-aching tiredness is then offset by flushes of adrenaline on stage, a sudden peak of nervousness, euphoria—a distinct up and down emotionally, physically, and mentally. Album touring has a special feeling too. People come to shows with expectations. Audiences have an idea of what you will play, how you will sound. They may even think they have an idea of who you are from the articles they've read and the meaning they unearthed in your lyrics. Sometimes when Chan was in one spot for a moment, her label would fax her reviews. She would read the verdict before providing another nightly opportunity to be judged again. Late at night, she would distract herself by working on covers alone in her hotel room. Covers became a warm blanket of familiarity, pushed and prodded with Chan's singular voice and vision.

Each night, Chan would drag between sagging handmade stages slathered in layers of black paint. Amps, ill-placed monitors, barely tuned pianos boiled under blinding stage lights that helped to slightly obscure the sea of colors and kids out on the floor along with the dense smog of cigarette smoke that lingered on clothes long after the club. The crowds were filled with a mix of late-90s-style apathy, fading grunge, the quietly aging ironic indie darlings, the occasional preppy who heard this was cool, and soft emo souls that intermingled, but a new crowd was also there. A new crowd of rabid fans armed with bulky digital cameras, cell phones, camcorders, and mini-disc recorders bubbled onto the scene. They were the strangers behind budding internet forums, hiding in the shadows to trap moments for posterity, criticism, a sense of community—a way to prove that they too lived and were alive. They could be there to bootleg the show and share it amongst another totally absent audience. Audiences could also be there simply for the music or maybe to fantasize about being, or being with, Chan. They could be there because the album resonated with some personal trauma expressed in song, real or imagined.

Chan mostly played with a band. Her backing members often took on stoic, rock personas: whammy bars and loose t-shirts hanging over skinny frames, slightly unbuttoned shirts, posturing pieced together from decades of male performers on album covers and in magazines. But Chan wasn't pretending to be on stage in the same way; it's like she was trying to figure out who she was supposed to be on stage. The honesty of her songs could make everyone (including herself) feel less alone, but the actual togetherness was awkward. She was at once inviting the spotlight and hiding from it. To deal with the enormity of this, she needed more barriers, barriers she made through long brown bangs, alcohol, mumbled self-deprecation, confusing stage presence, baggy clothes to hide under, an averted gaze unwilling to see the fans or trust the applause. Riders grew to include hard liquor and a case of beer or a bottle of tequila and a pack of Marlboros. Chan stood on stage night after night, absorbing a pulsing crowd of needs and wants.

Chan remained on the road with *Moon Pix* for months. She toured the United States and Europe. Then she did some sporadic US shows (one of which would follow the rest of her career) before heading to Australia. Even though she was in a hazy fishtank of touring, she made effort to connect with things outside of it. She would mail her rent dutifully to New York each month to secure the cheap apartment she kept before South Carolina; she would answer calls about her mother's health. She would send dozens of postcards to friends and family to remind them she was still out there. During her tour, Benjamin Smoke, an Atlanta radical poet whose creaky gothic-punk ballads grew alongside Chan's, passed away, another reminder of the fragility of life and the irreconcilable distances brought on by tour. Smoke's life would be immortalized in a documentary film a few years later that would be nominated for an Independent Spirit Award. The film posthumously spread his queer gospel even more than when he was alive.

On the twentieth anniversary of *Moon Pix*'s release, Chan Marshall returned to Australia and performed at the regal Sydney Opera House accompanied by a small string section, a flutist, Mick and Jim. She paused before coming to the stage. When she emerged, she wore a black velvet designer dress made by The Vampire's Wife, sparkles ruffled around the hem and sleeves. Her jewelry, most likely Chanel as she became a muse for Karl Lagerfeld in the late aughts, glinted mildly under the heavy lights. Her cat-eyeliner peaked out beneath her still shaggy bangs. Her face caught the lights from above, her brown boots firmly planted. She drank tea from a mug. There was no guitar to hide behind; she sang totally exposed. At the show's close, she spoke plainly, the newfound comfort in the spotlight making the ghosts recede into darkness and hinting at the distant memories of a South Carolina field: "Thank you all for accepting me. I don't know how many of you knew me when I was crazy. I'm sure there are people in the audience crazier than me. I hope you find the same blessings coming to you. It's good for us to take notice when we're doing well."

The same year, 2018, a film titled "Burden" premiered at the Sundance Film Festival. The film told the story of the friendship between Michael Burden, the co-founder of the KKK Museum/Redneck Shop in Laurens South Carolina, and David Kennedy, a Reverend and Civil Rights activist. Burden was a reformed Klansman who sold off his share of the building to Kennedy. He also once admitted to almost having assassinated the Reverend, his finger angled over a trigger aimed onto the street below where Kennedy walked, an action of so much weight and history now an anecdote in a newspaper article and in this book. In the film, Kennedy was played by Forest Whitaker, and Burden was played by model and actor Garrett Hedlund. The film was used for fundraising to transform the decaying Echo Theater—once the home to the hate-filled museum & gift shop—into something new: a community center to promote reconciliation and diversity. As the project's website says, "The Echo Project will redefine the story of the Echo Theater and Laurens into one of resiliency, justice, and hope. We hope to share the impact of that change with the world."

Stories are the distillation of memories—rounded, simple, clean—they can be made to conjure up warm nostalgia or painful pasts, none of which depict a real-life lived or what really happened. Sometimes there are truths buried deep within the fictions or representations, a glimmer of what was. But it is the retelling that lingers on, a porous memory smoothed with age and constantly viewed through different lives. Collectively, it is decided what parts of what stories will remain and what futures these stories can become.

2

He Turns Down

Chan on Recording *Moon Pix*

Amy: Who plays on the new album?
Chan: Mick Turner and Jim White from Dirty 3. You know
when you're packing for a trip and you don't know what
the weather's gonna be like? That's what it was like for
the two days we recorded.
                    Interview with Amy Kellner, Index, *1998*

Anthony: So what is it about this record that you hold dear
to, what is it that this record means to you?
Chan: … it's the first time I've really given a shit about
recording one. It's the first time I've really payed attention
in the studio. It's the first time I ever had an idea of what I
wanted. And it's the first time I've really liked all the songs.
And it's the first time I ever had a good time in the studio.
                    Interview with Anthony Carew (interview clip
                    unverified, re-posted on messageboard),
                    Gravity Girls, *1998*

Greg: Recording this album, were you in full control?

Chan: Absolutely. I was tellin' somebody it's like having thirty plates on each arm, and trying to shift them. Shifting like twenty plates to the other hand. That's what it was like, because we only had two days of recording time.

Interview with Greg Weeks, Sand
from the Urns, 1998

Chan: … then came the flute player … never heard my music, never heard the songs, "He Turns Down," she listens to it, goes out there, plays, and she's not really in it, she holds herself back, and I go "Stop-stop-stop!," and she's like "Is it horrible?" (laughs), and I was like "No, I just think you're holding back," so we have to turn up the song really loud in the headphones, and she has to play really loud or whatever to get her sound through, and then she came out, first recording, and that's the take! She was fucking great, she was so amazing.

Interview with Marcus Maida,
Hotel Discipline, 1998

cf: are you happy with it?
chan: I am cause I got to do things, I got to direct it a little. and the other times, we didn't do anything, we just pressed record. this time I got to branch out and figure out where I thought it should go …

Interview with Gail O'Hara, chickfactor, 1999

Matt Voigt on Recording *Moon Pix*

I was the house engineer at Sing Sing so I would be the guy that would record sessions if someone came in; I'd be one of the first people to be asked. I think Chan was out in Australia; she must have been visiting Mick and Jim and hanging out with them. I think she had her advance and needed to spend it and needed to deliver an album, so she asked for Jim's help. I don't know if she did some demos beforehand, but she just called up the studio and said, "Yeah, I'd like to book in some time." Kaj from Sing Sing called me and said, "Can you do the session?" I think she wanted to do New Years Day, and I was like, "Yeah, maybe not New Years Day." I don't know if it was ten days or twelve days. We just booked a block of time and met on January 2 and started. I'd never met Chan before. She just walked up to the studio—I think it was just Chan that came on the first day—and we just go: "What do you want to do? Let's start."

I was just there to capture her and not be judgmental and just to let her … to give her the confidence to perform and open up. When anyone performs, it's about opening up and sort of exposing yourself. The veils come down, and you perform. You hear honesty in recording, we detect honesty, and I think we're quite good at detecting it, and so if you have an honest—if you're really vulnerable and open, you're performing, and you're just giving it your all—then that comes through in the recording. So my role was really just to make her feel comfortable and just capture that, whatever happened. I wasn't there to mold the songs. I was just there to … It's like taking a photograph. You sort of have to become a little bit invisible. And I just did what I can to do that.

It's a moment in time because time changes, and you change along with it—your feelings and whatever you wanted to express change. So capturing in time you record these songs; two years down the track, and they're completely different—completely different emotions, everything's all different—it's all about just snapping it and capturing it.

I think she had a great bond with Jim, and she was really comfortable around Jim. He was like an advisor, a rock for her, I think. He gave her lots of confidence. He was like, "Yeah, this is great, this'll be great. It's all gonna be okay," it's always just, "Right, let's do it." It was good for me sometimes too because sometimes in the recording, there's part of me that was like, "This needs to be a bit tighter," and all that kind of stuff or, "This needs to be this way," and I'm trying to hold myself back and Jim's like: "That's it, that's great." And you're like, "Yeah, it is."

Obviously, it was really emotional for her to sing all those songs. And maybe she did feel anxious about the studio. I didn't ask her about that. She would not make it through the takes, then she'd stop and break down a little bit, and it would just be that reassurance that everything's ok, it sounds amazing—which it did because she has such an amazing voice. We'd get a take, and it's like, "I don't know how we can make that better. Let's do a double vocal, let's try some harmonies, let's put some colors." That album, for me, is like this raw emotion with just splashes of interesting color around it. I was listening to it yesterday, and I was thinking it's kind of like you're floating in an ocean, and it's storming outside, but then you put your head under the water, and there's all this activity happening, this color, there's fish swimming around and all this excitement. Little dabs of color.

Sing Sing is one big room, probably about 9 meters by 10 meters, or 11 meters by 10 meters, and then there's three isolation rooms at the back, and they're 4 meters by 3 meters and 5 meters by 3 meters. So, how did we have it …? We would have had … I remember I used an M49 as a vocal microphone which is an old Neumann valve microphone. I used a 1073 Neve mic pre—this is all the stuff I remember [laughs]—and I used a recently refurbished Fairchild 660 as a compressor. As far as a vocal chain, you couldn't go wrong. That's such a nice vocal chain. Probably just had an 87 and a 57 on the guitar amp, which was in one room, Chan was in another, and we just laid it down. I might have even opened up the door so she could get a bit of natural ambiance just so she could feel connected to the guitar and stuff like that.

Being a performer—not like a good performer—I know the feeling of when you perform in a room with instruments and other players; it's completely different than when you've got headphones on. And I really like the idea of capturing things naturally and having ambiance come through. That style of recording doesn't suit every style of music, but I quite enjoy the idea of recording like that, that natural vibe.

Jim organized the musicians. We did some songs where it was just Chan playing guitar and singing, and we captured that as one, and then Jim came in and recorded drums. I think "Cross Bones Style," Jim came in later and recorded drums on top. Then there were some other songs when the band came in and performed as a band. I think the flute was an overdub; I can't remember whether that was a live performance or an overdub; I'm not quite sure …? Oh, the thunder sample. When I listened to it last night, because I knew I did it, but when it happened, "O! Thunder! It was good, oh that's nice!" That was Chan's idea! Yeah, "so I want to get some thunder on here." "Okay, cool, let's find some thunder." So we had some sample library CDs, and we found some thunder, and we laid some thunder all over the song and then mixed in the bits that we thought were appropriate, yeah it worked well. It complements rather than try to take control or be the shining light, it's just a complement.

There's heaps of little moments. I love the drum tones on it. Back then, was it 1997? The drum room at Sing Sing was a bit different because they hadn't renovated the control room. The control was quite small, and the drum room was really big, and it has this distinct tone to me, and then it got changed in 1999; they extended the control room; the drum room became a bit smaller. For me, that's really nostalgic because I know that sound of the room, and I love it. I didn't realize we did so much experimenting with delays and things. That was cool, and I like how that turned out.

I just love the vocals on "No Sense" and how it kind of climbs up vocally, and the harmonies come in. It's just powerful to me. I like that for some reason. And I really like "Color and the Kids" too. I think that's the last thing we recorded. It was something that she was just like, "I'll put this down as well." It was just a little bit different, jumped on the piano, it was a live performance again, and that worked out well. Sometimes it's difficult recording a piano and a voice live because you can get some comb filtering and phasing in the microphones; maybe I had the lid down to stop all of that to make it nice and mellow? … Things did move around a bit, but we got creative with using delays and stuff to sort of blend it all together—I love that part in "American Flag" where she falls behind with the guitar and the voice a bit, and the lyrics are like "the American Flag falls behind" and it's perfect.

Another funny thing I remember is that when I started mixing it, so, I think on the first song, I'm adding things and equalizing things and compressing things, and then I asked Chan, "how's it sounding? What are you thinking?" She kind of thought for a bit, and then she grabbed a bit of paper, and she just drew this circle, like this circle [mimes intensely drawing a repeated circle, around and around]. And I was like, "Cool, I get it." It was too compressed, it was too encapsulated, and so I backed off all the compression and let things be a lot more open, and I was like, "Yeah, that's how it should be." That was cool. I loved that.

It wasn't a technical thing; it was like an emotional thing … if the emotion's not coming through and things are detracting from the emotion, then that's no good. So that's what we tried to do.

I remember saying to her at the end of the album, we were in the kitchen making a cup of tea or a coffee or something, and I said to her, "Chan, I just want to thank you for, you know, letting me record you, I've learned so much." And I think she looked at me a bit confused like, "You, what, learned how to record?" "No, I learned so much about myself. People get so hard on themselves, and I see that I do, and we get hard on ourselves, and we shouldn't be so hard on ourselves. We should love ourselves more." So that's where I was coming from, but I don't think she understood that's what I meant …

She's just such an honest and open person, and she's just got such a talent and a beautiful voice, and you just want to listen to it.

3

No Sense

Chan in New York

After Australia, Chan returned to New York City to prepare for the album's release. She first came to the East Village in July 1991 or '92 and then came back in August for good. She sat on a stoop on 4th St. with her friend whose boyfriend had just died; they drank margaritas and smoked cigarettes. They probably sat in that way you can only sit in New York, like the whole city block is a big house and doing nothing feels like doing something because the city lives its own life around you. Bikes were constantly stolen, fights broke out in the night, heroin flooded the streets, and everything was dirty. Both squatters and drug dealers would keep watch for criminals and the law.

People would live in the bones of buildings for free or cheap, hauling water up from fire hydrants when the pipes no longer worked. Chan found an affordable squat off Avenue B filled with Communists. Her bathroom was covered in graffiti. Her roommates had an evil street cat named Boyfriend brought in solely to kill the rats. When people died—from overdoses or other epidemics sweeping the city—their belongings would go to the sidewalk or thrift shops, scooped up by the living. Most of Chan's wardrobe came from the piles on the streets, her style born of necessity.

Chan's friend from Atlanta, Glen Thrasher, moved to New York around the same time she did. He had a respected music zine called *Lowlife*, and a radio show in Atlanta on WREK called Destroy All Music, which formed connections to the New York scene. Chan and Glen went to ABC No Rio on Rivington, an artist space with a perpetual loop of patching and decay. Layers of tags, paintings, grime covered up the facade to keep out the light and whatever else the space was girding itself against. Crowds were confusingly varied, on and off stage. Chan and Glen sat on folding chairs and watched a naked woman bathed in bright lights accompanied by a person banging on metal and a man playing a saxophone (maybe Anthony Braxton or Fishes & Roses). Chan discovered free jazz. There was a feeling of expression, of needing to get it out, whatever it was—no matter how rough or muddy or received. This appealed to Chan, whose Southern exposure to music might have been more uniform in its boy-guitar-stage or choir-organ-church formulations. There was something wild and free here but something also a little unhinged, the way your stomach drops out on the descent from a carnival ride. It gave Chan confidence to embrace imperfection.

Jobs traveled by word of mouth or through the thin weekly newsprint of *The Village Voice*. In need of work, Chan applied to be a stripper in the dirty version of Times Square.

She unloaded meat from trucks in the Meat Packing District. She waitressed uptown at 92nd and Madison, where she wore a tie. She organized the home of a woman with obsessive–compulsive disorder. She worked at Todd's Copy on Mott St. between Prince and Spring, the only place with a color printer in the neighborhood causing artists and musicians, like Jean-Michel Basquiat and John Giorno, to stream in, a place where Kim Gordon and Thurston Moore of Sonic Youth once worked. Eventually, Chan settled into a waitressing job at Moma's, a soul food restaurant in her neighborhood. A lucky few would get to work in music, at record stores like Other Music, Pier Platters or Kim's Underground, radio stations like WFMU, or See Hear, a tiny zine store nestled in between 1st & 2nd. A select handful were lifted from a single restaurant and recruited to work at a small indie record label called Matador, launched out of Chris Lombardi's apartment in 1989 and run alongside Gerard Cosloy—a label that eventually welcomed Chan and her music, in addition to other indie legends like Pavement and Liz Phair.

Like Matador, Max Fish opened in 1989, founded by artist Ulli Rimkus, who worked at Tin Pan Alley with other artists like Nan Goldin and Kiki Smith. The famous female-focused bar was in Times Square, then a place of debauched, local squalor. The Fish was on Ludlow St. and attracted artists and musicians moving to the area with a creative, homey haven in the desolate neighborhood. The bartenders were in bands; the drinkers were in bands; the soundtrack would be new releases from their bands. Most people had nicknames. Kittens were born in the bathroom, pieces of art covered the space, and were sometimes bartered for beer. Giant red polka dots against a glaring blue wall made for an iconic backdrop. The place became a hub for this particular indie scene, changing throughout the years as generations moved in and out. Tom Otterness and Elliott Smith gave way to Dash Snow and TV On The Radio.

Fashion designers moved into the neighborhood with a mix of crafty and edgy, followed by the fashionista squad with places like TG-170. Alleged Gallery opened on Ludlow, too, a space that elevated skate culture, launching the careers of artists like Shepard Fairey and Barry McGee. Collective Unconscious was also housed on Ludlow where it hosted an Anti-Slam, pushing back against the competitive poetry trend and broadcasting radical acceptance (and a lot of nudity).

Clubs emerged in the area too, a heaving, growing, throbbing list of places to play live music, see music, and be seen: Mercury Lounge, Fez, Brownies, Irving Plaza, Wetlands, Tramps, Spiral, The Cooler, The Pyramid, Continental Divide, Tonic, Thread Waxing Space, CB's 313 Gallery. The original CBGB's was on the Bowery. Its toxic bathroom seemed like a place made for shooting up. There was so much graffiti; it was hard to find the toilet. CB's & ABC No Rio had helped birth the NY No Wave scene in the 70s, an art-rock movement pushing against rock n' roll norms formed in the shadow of the Velvet Underground and ushering forth acts like Sonic Youth. Bands like Morphine and The Pixies from Boston and Sebadoh and Dinosaur Jr. from Massachusetts added an alt-rock tone to the air, a familiar rockness but tinted with a progressive, lo-fi sound. An accessible togetherness bonded the music scene tightly. Bands would wheel equipment across uneven sidewalks, carrying them into deep dark, cold sub-basement practice spaces. Studios could be rented by the hour or by the month, shared like people shared band members. Cat Power's first two albums were recorded in Sonic Youth's practice space on Mott St.

Living spaces doubled as studios, practice space, storage space, and production lines. Amps would crowd tiny living quarters, carried up and down flights and flights of stairs. Indie record labels sprung up regularly, mailing out CDs (which were becoming more affordable to produce by the week). Props for off-Broadway shows would annoy roommates. Indie film companies popped up in closets. Homemade zines would be manually stapled in a D.I.Y. assembly line. The whole scene ran on padded envelopes.

Michael in New York

Michael Galinsky showed up to his dorm room on East 10th in New York City with youthful energy, large glasses, and a head full of floppy curls. Toward the end of the '80s, he had traveled up from Chapel Hill, North Carolina, a place with an intense music scene and excellent college radio. His new roommate, a Junior named Pete Walsh, handed him a single from his band, Hypnolovewheel. The music was rooted in '60s rock with warm harmonies but preoccupied with a sweet avant-garde itch. Michael had tried to play music with friends in high school, but it never worked. He didn't view himself as a talented musician—his friends were much better—and their aesthetics clashed. Two guys living in the dorm room next door showed up soon after: one grew up in Chicago (his best friend was just about to start the record label Drag City) and the other was a record obsessive. The crew showed Michael all of the local record stores and clubs;

he was going to shows three or four nights a week in the blanket of venues that stretched from the East Village down into the Bowery. On his first day of sophomore year, Michael and Gene Booth (who would go on to be a publicist at Drag City and a music journalist) were going out to grab a beer and crossed paths with some kid in a Dinosaur Jr. t-shirt. They invited the newfound friend along. His name was Chris O'Rourke. Chris and Michael spent a year hanging out and sharing music.

In college, Michael studied religion, sociology, and anthropology, but photography had also been of interest. He took photos for his high school yearbook and newspaper and some for his college paper. He would spend time in photo bookstores flipping through the pages, including the greats: William Eggelston, Robert Frank, Gary Winogrand. When a band played on the roof of Brittany Hall at NYU, Michael took photos that ended up in a zine. Then, while visiting his girlfriend out on Long Island, he found the perfect subject for his color photo class project: the mall. So, in the Summer of his sophomore year, he set off across the country to photograph the American Mall, structures of capitalism and community that had become a vital part of society, a new kind of public square. Michael walked through malls all over the United States—North Dakota, California, Missouri—often taking shots with his Nikon FG-20 from the hip to avoid detection or intruding on scenes. It was like street photography moved indoors, asphalt replaced by this new plastic microcosm of fountains, fluorescent lights, stone washed-denim, and hairspray, moments in time that would otherwise be forgotten.

When he came back to college for his Junior year, Chris and Michael naturally started a band with Chris' RA, Racheal McNally, on drums. They would practice in the basement of their dorm two or three nights a week, learning and developing their music together. They started to play shows, convincing club owners to take a chance, piling enough friends into a venue to be invited back to play again. Slumberland records put out their first album, followed by two records with Homestead Records, a label where Gerard Cosloy worked prior to Matador and where he first met Chris Lombardi who worked at an affiliated label, Dutch East Trading Co. Michael's band was called Sleepyhead.

On Sleepyhead's first tour, they headed South. They rolled up to a venue in Knoxville, Tennessee, called the Snake Snatch Lodge. They went around back to an alley hemmed in by brick buildings to load in where another band on the bill, Boondoggle, had just finished unloading. Michael took a picture of them. They took a picture of Michael. Versus from New York showed up next. They all played their sets to a near-empty room. They drank cheap PBR, the bartender cleared their tab and threw them some cash even though little money was made that night. They didn't know where they were going to stay, but a guy who worked at a pizza place showed up, and the bartender asked if he could put them up:

"How many?"
(counts on fingers) "13?"
"Okay."

They were learning how to be a band while living the life of one. Each show was the equivalent of fifteen practices. This small Southern lo-fi scene felt akin to the New York one, but it wasn't contained in a few city blocks. It was a similar collection of outsiders with unimpeded creativity and even though they would commune with bands passing by on tour, the slight isolation made for a purer, coarser expression. The indie rock scene wasn't just about slacker stylings, it was also about testing out other ways to be. It was about figuring out how to make communities bound together by things other than stuff.

When Sleepyhead made it back to New York, Michael felt inspired to document the scene he just experienced. He tried to convince his girlfriend (and eventual wife and ongoing collaborator), Suki Hawley, to drop out of film school and come with him to make a film, hoping to document it before it faded away. Suki had become addicted to film editing as a teen. After undergrad, she spent a brief time in the editing room of B-movie, Sexploitation master Roger Corman in Los Angeles and then headed to New York to continue film school. For a semester, she interned at Apparatus Productions, Barry Ellsworth, Christine Vachon, and Director Todd Haynes' non-profit company that produced Todd's first film, *Superstar: The Karen Carpenter Story*. Suki was also an assistant to the director on the 1995 film *Party Girl*, the first film to ever play on the internet. It was during this job that Michael tried to lure her into the director's chair.

At first, she was reluctant, but after following her roommate's band, Ruby Falls, down South, she immediately saw what Michael saw: it was about capturing something before it died; before it was destroyed. Suki dropped out of film school. Michael got a small advance from Matador records to make the film; the soundtrack featured Matador artists. Michael and Suki wrote the script, and Suki directed. The script was primarily memories from tours past—the lack of food and free beers, the midnight conversations in a stranger's kitchen, the sitting and waiting—acted out by the band Rodan. The theft of a van was added after Michael's father read the script providing one single note: "Where the fuck's the conflict?" They went with a small crew to shoot across Louisville, Nashville, and Chattanooga for ten days. The result was *Half-Cocked* (1994), a gritty indie film about gritty indie music. It feels slightly at home with *Clerks* (1994) and *Kids* (1995), movies with mostly non-actors documenting subcultures before they were wiped out by time or money or adulthood. About a week after the grueling film shoot, Sleepyhead went on tour with Yo La Tengo. During that tour, Kurt Cobain killed himself.

A year later, in 1995, Michael was hanging out in his friend Tim Foljhan's apartment in New York, and Chan Marshall was there. She had started playing and recording with Steve Shelley and Tim (both in the band Two Dollar Guitar; Steve was also the drummer for Sonic Youth). Suki and Michael were touring around *Half-Cocked*, connecting it to audiences the way they knew how, through small shows and rock clubs. Michael was about to drive up north with Suki to Wesleyan in Connecticut to screen their film, and Chan was about to play a solo show up there. She asked if she could get a ride. While stopped at a gas station Chan hopped out of the van. Michael took her photo. She looked like a young, bright-eyed drifter in an oversized coat with her unplugged guitar in hand.

Headlights were spotlights; a dirty gas station was her stage. Michael's photographs crystallized the community around him. The happenstance and the intentional, the details and the bigger picture, Michael knew how history could be made and how quickly history could be lost.

From a Conversation with Michael Galinsky

What helped me even to think that there was some relevance in taking photographs was that I met those people on my very first day of college. A couple days later, I met Mike McGonigal, who had a magazine called *Chemical Imbalance*, and he was like, "sure I'd love your pictures." Yo La Tengo played on our roof, and I gave him some of those pictures; those are some of the first music pictures I ever had published. From then on, I would give him lots of pictures. It gave me some sense of outlet. I was taking pictures of bands before I was in a band, and once I was in a band, I started taking even more, and then my band started to play, and I would start to take pictures of the bands we played with.

Even in the context of the mall stuff … I had mostly taken sociology, religious studies, and anthropology classes in my first two years. So when I took my first photo class in the end of my second year, it was really thinking in the context of documentation, noticing details that will mean something later, what does this say about Community, etc … When I started taking pictures, I was also aware of just how important it was to document things that would mean something later, and, at the time, not everything at every event that happens means something later, but if an event means something later and there's no documentation it loses some of its power … I was like, "Okay, this is our scene. Someone needs to document it." So if there are two or three people taking pictures, I wouldn't bother because it didn't feel important, somebody's got that because film was expensive and I didn't have that much access to dark rooms. I didn't shoot all that much, but I did start trying to take pictures of most of the people we played with if I liked them, if I thought they were good [laughs]. Or if I cared, if it felt necessary.

This was before the internet mostly, so I thought they would be in books. When people write about this stuff, there's going to need to be images. When people make documentaries, there's going to need to be images. I knew that there was value in them, and I didn't know what that value would exactly be, but I was also using the time. I did a lot of photographs for *Puncture Magazine, Signal to Noise, Tape Op*, and the K Records catalog. My role is a part of an ecosystem that is self-sustaining. That's really what it was.

*

… I actually started to write an idea for a museum show called "Underground from the Inside," and it was about all these people like myself who were documenting the scene as part of the community. You have Pat Graham in DC who then went to Olympia and was doing that stuff. You have Pat Blashill down in Austin documenting all of that, like Poison 13 and Butthole Surfers, and you had Bill Daniel doing similar stuff. You had this photographer Marty Perez in Chicago documenting the scene. It was like they were part of the community, and then if someone needed images, they would come to that person, but the person wasn't like, "I'm doing this because I'm going to sell this image." They're doing it because it's a part of what we're doing, and so it's a different aesthetic idea—even if there are different aesthetics to the way the people shot the images—the force of it was: "I'm a part of something. I'm not doing this to feed on this community. I'm a part of this community."

… When we made the movie *Half-Cocked*, it's not a documentary. It is a document, and it's not a documentary. Partly because of some misguided sense of what a documentary is allowed to be. Having studied anthropology and sociology, I kept having this colonial idea of critical distance: you can't document something unless you have critical distance. So we might have made a documentary, but part of it is I can't make a documentary because I'm a part of it. I can document it, but I can't make a documentary so let's make a narrative that is collaborative. Later on, I was like: that's a total bullshit concept. In some ways, you can't really make a documentary unless you have a deep connection to the community. Then that gets complicated in other ways …

… When Occupy happened, I saw a lot of these videos that started right away. And I thought those are interesting, and they feel like propaganda, let me go down there and see what it is. I agreed with what they were doing, but they felt like they were activist videos … So I went to look at it, and then I started taking pictures, and I started asking people questions. The first piece I made was mostly photos but just talking to people asking, "Why are you here?" By the time I went around, other people were asking around the park why they were there. The people who were asking the questions were now holding the signs twenty minutes later because, "Oh, that's why I want to be here. Okay, I am here. I'm part of this." It can happen that quickly, in that moment. But I started making a lot of pieces about Occupy, and the idea was it was in between advocacy and what we would call journalism. Where journalism is explaining it in a misguided attempt to understand it, and activism is explaining it, I would say, in a slightly misguided attempt to sell it. So what's in between? How do people get to make up their own minds?

*

I think Sonic Youth was probably playing with image almost as an artistic concept: what does this even mean, and what role do we play? There's an interesting Sonic Youth video; Phil Morrison did a bunch of videos for one record—we did one for Swimsuit Issue where we all just got drunk and didn't wear shirts and smoked a bunch in my friend's apartment—but there's another one where they're practicing in their practice space, and they turn into Hypnolovewheel, or Hypnolovewheel turns into them. It's weird, another kind of concept about what is identity, they play kind of similar music, are they the same thing? That was much more about art in the same way maybe The Flaming Lips were. Nirvana were in this weird middle space where they just tried to be who they were, and they said, "fine, we want people to hear us," just as, say, the Talking Heads wanted people to hear them, "we'll be a part of this machine." But, even in the early '90s, Nirvana got caught up in something that was beyond even their ability to envision. I think that was crushing and overwhelming because they were so intent on being pure, in a way, and that was impossible …

… In some ways, it's a conversation about what is art. I feel like [the *Moon Pix* album cover] was [Chan] stepping into some kind of sense of power in her own work and being in control of it, rather than being hidden (like hiding behind her hair), and I think that was a conscious decision. I think I would look at that less as marketing than art as a sense of identity and art as a way to explore identity. And an interest in fashion and culture, and what those mean—no different than The Rolling Stones in some ways. In fact, I think her cover of "Satisfaction" is so amazing because it helps you feel those lyrics on this really deep level that made me go, "Oh my God! I listened to that song a million times. I never understood how fucking brilliant those lyrics are." She made me understand that. She's an incredible artist who turned her identity into part of her art. I guess part of it is that—if you're looking at it in kind of capitalistic terms, etc.—marketing is a problem. If you're not looking at it as marketing but as a way to explore identity and get people to think more deeply about identity, then it's actually like Sonic Youth on DGC. It's a way to have a bigger platform for discussing these ideas. I would fault it when that identity gets so lost in "how am I going to sell more," and it becomes overwhelmed by marketing rather than activating marketing as part of an artistic endeavor, and I think there's a clear difference …

… I sent Chan a note the other day saying I just applaud you for using your platform every day to focus on really important issues and not from a preachy level but saying: "Hey, you should pay attention to this, and I have a megaphone."

Figure 3.1 Chan Marshall en route to a show at Wesleyan
University, 1995. Photograph by Michael Galinsky (1 of 2)

Figure 3.2 (2 of 2)

Roe in New York

In 1997 or 1998, photographer Roe Ethridge was living in Williamsburg, Brooklyn, the next stop for many LES residents who were being displaced by a sudden influx of money (and a neighborhood that became the next forefront for gentrification). Before Roe Ethridge moved from Atlanta to New York, he would visit the city and sleep on the couch of his old art school classmate Cindy Greene. Cindy went from Atlanta to the Art Institute of Chicago, where she most likely met Casey Spooner, her New York roommate. Spooner was one-half of the band Fischerspooner, while Greene was one-half of the soon-to-be fashion label Libertine, both gritty glam in their distinct ways. Roe would go on to make many images of Fischerspooner, building their brand through pictures at a time when brand and life were yet to fully merge. His work as a catalog photographer in Georgia helped him see the strange lines between art and ad, life and performance, lines he erased in one of his first commercial shoots, "How to Put On Lipstick," for *Allure* magazine.

Roe was hired by a French art director who no longer cared about their job, hoping that hiring someone with little to no fashion experience would help them get fired. Roe consulted photobooks "how do you do beauty lighting?" Kathryn, an Australian model, arrived at the studio with hazel eyes and straight, brown hair. Her skin bright and smooth, but her lips were peeling, chapped against the harsh, chilled city winds. Nervous and out of his element,

Roe told a joke to lighten the mood; the model laughed, he snapped a photo, her blank exterior broken for a moment. When a version of the image was printed in the magazine, her lips were airbrushed to perfection. When the image hung on the wall of the 2000 Greater New York show at MoMA's P.S. 1 in Long Island City, the lips were chapped and uncomfortable.

In August or September of '98, Chan Marshall called Roe, "we should take a picture, maybe we can do something for the album cover." In Georgia, Roe knew the elusive Chan as a teen; both worked at different locations of the same local pizza chain. Her perceptive charm behind the counter with a cigarette dangling between her lips made him, and nearly all other indie rock boys, blush.

His apartment was stifling hot as many loft spaces skirted laws; things like ventilation and fire code safety were, and still are, a luxury. His roommate had moved out suddenly, leaving behind her belongings, including the image-conscious wardrobe of a young Brooklynite. The pile of clothes Chan picked through for their photo session was an upgrade from her utilitarian curb-fashion. A classic denim jacket was chosen, slightly oversize, worn with holes in a way that was seen as "deconstructed," not broken or used. Fake silken magnolias driven up by Roe during a visit home were propped from above, resting or clamped in place somehow. Chan took position under the blossoms.

Roe shot in Polaroid Type 64, a large format film that gives a near instant negative and positive. He took one shot, two shots—the flash producing even more focused light to the already oppressive heat. Chan stared off in the distance, lips slightly parted, hand slightly raised with a sense of anticipation, wonder, maybe even horror. An emergent glow bounced off her skin against a black background, kind of like the day for night effect used in movies where daylight pretends to be its opposite. After the second pull of the shoot, Roe said, "Do you know what this is?" Chan replied in a whisper, "Yes."

@roeethridge

Images on The Internet

In the '90s, the internet was still attached to a location: the one person in the neighborhood whose family had a computer, the local library, the internet cafe with terrible coffee. You had to go to and get on the internet. Computers were physically connected to the real world through phone lines, as was—and still is—much of their iconography: a tiny floppy disk meant save, a little trash can delete. AOL instant messenger provided little popup windows to communicate with strangers, mimicking the sound of a creaky door opening and shutting to signal someone's entrance or exit.

Some sites tried to mimic a real-world understanding of space with grids along axes. Other sites abandoned all sense of order; background and foregrounds fought for supremacy through jagged little pixels. Some sites left rough-hewed gifs floating in space, nothing to ground them, a confusing, weightless loop of movement or gesture. Drop shadows were abundant, suggesting sources of light from all angles. Backgrounds to websites were often tiled images. Many didn't scale properly, leaving one with a headache-inducing puzzle mixed with skewed images that no one knew how to size correctly. The fonts and colors were limited, but monitors varied so widely that it didn't even matter. It was an entirely new medium with tons of possibility but in such infancy that it didn't know how to walk just yet, like the creepy CGI baby on the TV show *Ally McBeal* (which aired the same week *Moon Pix* was being recorded). The focus was still on the content and the technology, not just the way the content looked.

It was the perfect place for fan culture to rise as people began to connect around nodes of mutual understanding found through the limited search functions and hubs. Usenet (a pre-world-wide-web networking system) gave way to listservs, message boards, chatrooms, and other forum-like formats with text-heavy rows of topics and responses. Some were invite-only, some were official, some were unofficial. Very distinct strata of fandoms started to emerge as one chose where to go or why/how they would cede from an existing digital space to make their own. How the early web siloed and splintered networks of music fans should have been a warning of its isolating power.

Suddenly, every entity knew they had to have a website to access people and money. Matador Records site came to be in the late '90s. It was rudimentary, a few images, some text, with a red navigation menu scaled up the side: News, Matador Info, *¡Escandalo!* (Matador's print promotional newsletter, strongly labeled "not a zine"), Bands, Buy Stuff,

Site Index. They had lyrics, interviews, and tour dates and also relied on others for content, providing links to freshly coded fan sites, chipping at the barrier between fan and band. Matador linked out to these sites often with commentary on each, "the first and best fan page, methinks," "Are the lyrics correct? Lots of pictures. Sorta eerie, for no one reason." Chan-centric messageboards and fan clubs also arose, but archives on these are hazy, and insular fan communities continue to love the veil of usernames.

As people began scanning their film camera output and digital cameras were becoming more accessible, the lag between album release or show & site narrowed (*Pitchfork* was founded in 1995). Mini DV and consumer camcorders were also around. An audience member could capture the show from their distinct point of view and share it on elaborate, growing virtual bootleg trading sites. MP3 and minidisc recorders could make much better sounding recordings. The quality improved overnight, moving from tapes to digital tapes to CDs and eventually to MP3s surfacing on places like Napster (founded in 1999) and, later, Limewire (2000). Digital recording and listening quietly revolutionized and desocialized, fundamentally altering music forever; a small part in a cosmic digital shift that would fundamentally alter all forms of storytelling forever.

4

Say

A Music Video

Long Island City, Queens, sits on the banks of the Gowanus canal, a filthy waterway so full of muck that it has tested positive for STDs. The side streets are mostly brick warehouses, each with an output (a donut factory, a piano manufacturer, a world-renowned contemporary art museum, artist studios, art car studios). One particular building was once a bread company, pumping out flour until 1983 when it then became Silvercup Studios, a large commercial film studio. *When Harry Met Sally, Working Girl,* and *Do the Right Thing* preceded Cat Power's video for "Cross Bones Style." In 1998, Director Brett Vapnek called in favor upon favor, picking up her phone and asking for help. Somehow she landed this supreme space, complete with lighting rig, to film *Moon Pix*'s one and only "dance track."

Brett studied experimental film at Hampshire College in Massachusetts near the Connecticut River—a place without grades, or majors, an academic playground for the liberal arts curious. It's a place that has pumped out many other notable creatures like Ken Burns and Elliott Smith. After college, Brett wandered over to New York to intern at the then start-up Matador Records. She stayed on in publicity, befriending musicians and slowly making a modest name in music videos for acts like Spoon and Helium. She met Chan in the office during her first album, *What Would the Community Think*, and directed the video for the track "Nude as the News" (a fan favorite that would go on to be screamed at Chan as a request forever, odd only because the song is said to be about her abortion).

The video for "Nude as the News" was made during a Summer program at Bard College which overlooks the Hudson River in Northern New York. It was shot on a Bolex using reversal film that can be developed without the need to process negatives or additional prints. It's a grainy black & white video, playing with time and lights. Chan's round baby-face framed by short bangs appeared silently mouthing words, singing, playing in the shadows. In one scene, she repeatedly opens a closet to find wire hangers and single articles of clothing, suggesting the missing people in the song's cryptic lyrics. Chan wears T-shirts & button-downs, adding an androgynous appeal as silhouettes of men and women and bugs on strings float by. Lights bounce around against a curtain made of mylar. It reminds a bit of the film *Boy Meets Girl* by Leos Carax, a raw post-French New Wave where jump cuts meet punk: scratches, noise, superimposition, camera flares, with soft planes of emotion living within each frame. Brett's sister was the art director/artist; she made the cutout puppets seen in shadows of the video, a shadow of her curls can be seen in a shot. No other crew was present. Brett edited the 16mm film on a flatbed and sliced, taped and sliced, taped and sliced. At the time, there were limited outlets for airplay. Music labels would rely on MTV (*120 Minutes* with Matt Pinfield was a reliable source for indie images), MTV2 (the sister station that became the place for music video content as the original MTV veered deeper into the reality TV genre), and a small host of cable access TV. The shortlist of outlets was gathered together in a list by Brett at Matador with tapes dutifully sent out in sturdy envelopes.

Brett eventually enrolled in Tisch School of the Arts at NYU—a place that pumped out Jim Jarmusch, Spike Lee, and Martin Scorsese. Her crew for "Cross Bones Style" were her NYU classmates, budding filmmakers hugging the new, fresh indie spirit (Jarmusch) but secretly pining for that possibility of Hollywood fame (Scorsese) that many NYU film students seem to silently crave. One of Brett's classmates who worked on her set that day was her future husband.

Before coming to film, Chan and Brett talked about what the video would be. Chan expressed a hesitant interest in lip-syncing. Lip-synching was not the indie-rock norm at a time but Brett and Chan came of age in the early Madonna years; her lip-synched "Lucky Star" video presented a female icon who was something cool and sexy, someone who signaled a sense of total control. There was comfort in the nostalgia and a tacit positioning within a tradition of female performers looking for an alternative to acting as oiled-up props in videos.

A group of Chan's friends were gathered as dancers. Brett Vapnek's sister was promoted from "mover of things" to dancer in a leather miniskirt. Another woman was the girlfriend of Matt Sweeney, the lead singer of Chavez. Another was an original LES fashion scenester who worked at the boutique TG-170. Another dancer was a music journalist. The women wore all black with slight variations: long pants, boot cut pants, a skirt, long shorts, a spaghetti-strapped tank top, a turtleneck, one had a wink to Madonna with a single, black lacey glove ruffled around the cuff. All of the women looked like normal human beings. Jim White wasn't available for the shoot, so a prop drummer was found. Harry Drudz, a bartender and drummer (and an original fixture at the bar Max Fish), played along. He wore a simple T-shirt, jeans, boots, a slightly studded belt peeked around his waist when shot from behind. On his bass drum, a sticker of the Lorax sat quietly in protest. A long fabric-covered cord, red or orange, connected Chan's Silvertone to a Fender amp, draped with a faded American flag.

Chan chose her clothes, two outfits—one a short-sleeved black button-up with a militaristic feel, blue jeans, alternating bare feet, and black, orange-wheeled roller skates, another remnant of her childhood. The other costume was a fitted red dress, and a classic bright blue bandana tied loosely around her neck. Her hair fell across her face, what would become her signature bangs started to take shape. She wore yellow nail polish and thin black bracelets reminiscent of Madonna on both arms. A single silver ring caught the light. Each detail was touched with awareness.

The background was a horizon-less expanse of white, a disorienting open space with clean lines against a pristine background, and a focus on movement. The indie spirit of the set felt honest, sensuous, and accessible. The dancers' eyes slightly darted off-screen, not knowing where to look, not used to being in front of a camera. The slight shimmer of lip gloss, the wild, slow-motion tossing of a backup dancer's hair, leather, rubber, bare feet—the set felt warm and human while being simultaneously chic and stark.

Everyone was forced to the other side of the building when Chan performed. Brett and Chan were alone, free from eyes and second guesses. Chan placed her world in front of Brett's camera, trusting Brett with her image. It was a turning point for Chan; she was announcing herself as a figure to be looked at, but on her terms, through eyes she chose. Shooting on film meant no instant results. One worked hard to set up shots hoping that they would get what they desired, but there was no immediate way of knowing if things were working.

Brett and Chan worked together on the choreography. Chan brought the hand gestures; Brett elaborated with a series of simple line dance steps. Something about the moves felt ritualistic: a bowing down, an opening of arms, hands in prayer, each limb positioned with exactitude. The moves felt like they were indirectly fighting against the sexist synchronized "Macarena" from a few years prior, the bubblegum confusion of the Spice Girls "girl power," and something slightly less spikey than what the riot grrrls had to offer. Chan brought her hands together in a gun position, a slow movement of shooting across the screen, these movements the only inkling of the song's origins.

"Cross Bones Style" was inspired by orphans Chan met on a beach in Cape Town, South Africa, young people whose parents were killed in diamond mines or as freedom fighters, kids moving between adulthood and childhood with unnatural ease. Like most of Chan's work, her voice captured the tenacity of the imbalanced world she witnessed but, with this album, she was slowly learning how to use image to do the same.

Comments Section

Roller boogie Chan is dope!

Avant-garde yoga class.

I was disappointed none of these women had hairy armpits.

A feminist tv commercial?

This MADE me buy yellow nail polish.

I bought my girlfriend yellow nail polish because of this video … looking back, that's kind of creepy.

Wait, that's Cat Power?! She's gorgeous! I've known of her since I heard her stuff ages ago, not what I was expecting.

I had this on VHS.

Saw this on MTV2 in '98, fan since.

The most compelling music video IMHO.

When I watch this video my heart cracks, I feel like a kid buying *Moon Pix* again.

From a Conversation with Director Brett Vapnek on Directing "Cross Bones Style"

I worked at Matador for two and a half years. I started there in '95, January of '95? I've actually known Chris [Lombardi of Matador] for a long time because my sister dated him in high school. He was a friend of mine, and I had just moved to New York after college in '94, trying to find a job, and couldn't. I studied experimental film and modern dance at Hampshire College … I was thinking I was going to somehow go into "Dance Films." I'm going to get a job working on "Dance Films"—that doesn't exist.

I would stop by Matador to visit Chris. I'd leave with a pile of CDs and a roll of the incredibly cool posters Mark Ohe was designing. At that time, Pavement's *Crooked Rain* had come out (and was blowing up) and Liz Phair's *Exile in Guyville* had just come out (and was blowing up). Matador was suddenly going from being a very small indie label to one with artists getting national mainstream attention. The press was really exploding. Chris was like, "why don't you come and work here for a month as an intern because we need help, it's crazy." There were only probably like twelve people working there total. So that's how I started. I was only going to be there for a month. I loved all of the musicians, and I loved being there. It was super fun. They offered me a job in publicity, and I ended up staying.

It was a great opportunity for me since I wanted to make music videos. I met a lot of musicians, and I ended up working with several bands from Matador. It was very much a scene. I mean, everybody went to all the shows and hung out with the bands; that was the fun part of working there … Chris and Gerard were so good at finding musicians with the potential for long careers. I was continually in awe of their ability to pluck bands out of relative obscurity.

*

I look back at the early Cat Power albums and remember Chan in the early days. How much she changed in terms of her image … *Moon Pix* was kind of the first turning point. When I look at that cover, I remember we were all kind of like, "Oh, wow, it's kind of glamorous!" She hadn't been on the cover of her other albums, and she was very tomboyish, extremely self-conscious, and so it was like she was kind of stepping out.

I remember hearing Cat Power for the first time and just thinking, "Oh God, she sounds a bit on the edge." I was nervous to meet her because I thought, "Oh my God, she's gonna be depressive, and it's going to be really hard to get her to go in front of the camera." But her personality was the opposite of what I expected. She was hilarious, super outgoing, had millions of friends, and made friends everywhere she went. She was totally charming, just so lovable. But also, in those days, she was very unsure of herself. She was definitely pushing herself out of her comfort zone to perform and make videos. She was just so talented—people were responding to it.

"Cross Bones Style" was this turning point where she came to me and said, "I think I want to lip-sync," which was like, "Oh, my God," because nobody was doing that in indie videos. It was kind of considered cheesy. But I thought it was an exciting idea. Almost immediately I came up with the concept of doing a take-off on Madonna's "Lucky Star" video. Chan and I are almost the same age, and we grew up with Madonna. Madonna's first record came out when we were in junior high, and that "Lucky Star" video was so iconic to us. It was when Madonna was authentic and cool. She had more of an underground club vibe when she first started out.

*

It was a different time than it is now. Now it's easy for people to shoot and cut their own stuff—the equipment and editing software is so accessible. But, in those days, it wasn't accessible at all. To learn how to shoot film, you had to go to school, where they had professional cameras, flatbed editing equipment, and film projectors!

The videos were so low budget I usually worked for free, and I got other people to work for free. The minuscule budgets went toward buying film and post-production. I pulled so many favors because I loved the artists, and I loved the music. I wanted to make videos that underscored how great the songs were.

I would usually pitch some ideas, and generally, once the idea was agreed on, it was what we were doing. With Chan and with Sleater Kinney, particularly, maybe with Mary—not so much Mary Timony but a little bit—it was also about them kind of trusting me to help them look good. I generally felt like people were leaning on me because they trusted my taste, my style … This is publicity, and a lot of these indie artists were coming from a different place than, obviously, Christina Aguilera or whatever. They're not like, "I have this polished, sexy beautiful image." It was more, "I'm a musician, but I don't want to look bad on film."

5

Metal Heart

A Statement

…Cat Power and Smog fans alike have pored over both artists' post-breakup albums (Moon Pix *and Smog's* Knock, Knock) *for clues to what exactly happened. While neither record draws the listener a map, each adheres to the same loose theme: two strong-willed, independent personalities coming to terms with the fact that as much as they'd like to, they aren't ready to settle down.*

Elizabeth Goodman, Cat Power:
A Good Woman, *2009*

*

Chan on Her Relationship

C: *A friend of mine, Tony, my old drummer, told me … "You should go & see this guy Smog"…*

we were walking to this concert & I had no idea what it was, I wasn't interested at all, just basically totally depressed … & then he started singing & I could hear those lyrics & I just got so happy, I felt like he was my peer or something … cause everybody else that was around that I've met, all these old but no-wave-music-New-York-type-older-people just totally intimidated me, I never talked to anybody … he's got a new record coming out called Knock Knock. Isn't that cool?

Chan Marshall interviewed by Marcus Maida,
Hotel Discipline, 1998

Greg: *How much of a help was Bill? He moved with you …
    was that as a friend or something more than that …?*
Chan: *Total companion.*
Greg: *And he helped you work through all that kinda'
    stuff?*
Chan: *Bill taught me something. I understood something
    new because of what he taught me.*

Interviewed by Greg Weeks, Sand from the Urns
(interview clip unverified, re-posted on personal blog), 1998

"That was my first," Marshall says plainly—and what she means is that, at 25, dating Callahan marked the first time that she had ever been in love.

"I never had a boyfriend," she insists. "I had someone that I recognized as my boyfriend when I was 18, I guess, but he didn't respect me at all. Yeah, that was the first one. I thought it was real. I don't know." Marshall begins to grin. "He was a great, wonderful person."

Interviewed by Trevor Kelley, Trevorkelley's Blog, From the Archives *(originally appeared in* Harp Magazine*), 2005*

Bill on His Relationship

Bill Callahan: I was kind of a little putz. Inchoate. Wandering. I didn't know how to be honest with myself and others…You can slip through the cracks and have a lot of adventures for a long time and when you get older you wonder if that was good for you, necessary, or a waste. I had an extended youth where I was waiting for someone to tell me what was up. I had to figure it out myself after many self-inflicted blows to the head. My relationship with Chan had recently ended.

…I wrote pretty much all of that album on the drive from South Carolina to Chicago.

Interviewed by Tim Scott, Vice, *2017*

Interviews with the Author's Ex-Boyfriends about Breakup Album Legends

Ted: *Pet Sounds* is one that I thought of that I knew was a breakup album. Another one is the most recent Radiohead album, *Moon Shaped Pool*. I knew those two were breakup albums, but then beyond that, I can't think of anything that I know is a breakup album …

Donna: How did you learn that *Moon Shaped Pool* and *Pet Sounds* were breakup albums? I'm interested in how we find these things out, the way these stories travel.

Ted: I've been out of the Radiohead loop for a long time when *Moon Shaped Pool* came out. When the album came out, I looked into what they were doing, and one of the things Thom Yorke was doing was getting divorced. Within like a year or so before that album came out, he got divorced, and I think she actually passed away not long afterward because she had cancer, I think.

Donna: Oh, that's horrible.

Ted: I don't know if there's any connection whatsoever to those two things, but he definitely got divorced right before that album came out. I don't know *Pet Sounds* to specifically be a breakup album, but that's just what everybody always says about *Pet Sounds*; it's just common wisdom. Specifically, I remember—do you remember the guy who worked at Danny's Pizza named Jeremy who was really into indie rock? Do you remember him at all?

Donna: Not really. I remember you talking about him. I only went inside Danny's Pizza twice?

Ted: Well, I remember him telling me that he had a girlfriend that he used to listen to *Pet Sounds* with, and they would sort of act out the songs, and it was about breaking up and getting depressed and then when "God Only Knows" comes on that's the narrator killing himself. He did this dramatic—like, ironic but dramatic—play that they put on while listening to *Pet Sounds*. So that's probably where it first came to my attention that it was a breakup album.

Donna: That's kind of cute in a sick way.

Ted: Yeah … it certainly is. I mean, that album can be pretty depressing.

Donna: It's definitely rough. One that I always knew as a breakup album that people talk about is *Rumours*.

Ted: I was gonna bring that one up too.

Donna: That's the one that people are always like: "I know exactly what this is about!"

Ted: I think it's just in the general wisdom that that is a breakup album because Fleetwood Mac is known for having relationship issues in their band—if there's one thing they're known for, it's that. I think it's clear in the songs and on a personal level. I think of that album when I think of my parents breaking up. Because I knew, even as a child, that that was a breakup album and that the people in this band had terrible relationships with each other and I sort of used to imagine something along the lines of my parents doing what was said in the songs. My brain connected the two things as if this album was about my parents breaking up. I remember wishing that my parents would at least make an album if they were going to break up.

Donna: How old were you when they broke up?

Ted: Nine, I guess? 8, 9? I just always knew that that was a thing with Fleetwood Mac, that it's about breaking up and divorce and terrible relationships and stressful relationships.

*

Brian: You know, I don't really think about breakup albums because I try not to associate music with girls because I hold the music I love very sacred … But to answer your question, New Order's *Technique* can be considered a breakup album of sorts. I believe Bernard

Sumner was going through a divorce with his wife at the time and was partying it up in Ibiza to deal with it. *Technique* is one of my favorite albums, and I listen to it year after year.

Donna: How did you learn he was going through a divorce?

Brian: In the early days of the internet, I would have read New Order fan pages. More recently, I've read a bunch of books about Joy Division/New Order, including both Hook's and Sumner's autobiographies. I'm still waiting for the Morris/Gilbert joint autobiography ... I want it to be super teched-out and geeky. Like a whole chapter devoted to the animal sounds they sampled. I guess what drew me to the album initially was the somber pain of the lyrics juxtaposed against that sort of hedonistic acid house vibe that was going on at the time that they helped pioneer. They pioneered so many musical and technological innovations that they never even cared to take credit for.

Donna: Breakup albums can be such a new sound or direction for an artist like they are mourning the person they were to become something new ... can synths be mournful? I guess animal sounds could be mournful?

Brian: ....I like what you said about the mourning the old person to become the new. I think that's a perfect metaphor for the transition from Joy Division to New Order. I was reading somewhere once that the band immersed themselves in disco and the lifestyle to cope with Ian's death. So I always think there's this sense of mournfulness in Sumner's lyrics, no matter how hedonistic they try to be. I do think that synths can be mournful if infused with the soul of the operator. As far as animal sounds go, I think they sampled some sheep on "Fine Time"? But the best animal sample is the frog solo on the video version of "The Perfect Kiss" off of *Low Life*. Apparently, it was so complex that they had to stop playing the song when they updated their equipment because they couldn't reproduce it. Also, in "The Perfect Kiss" video, Peter Hook is rocking sweatpants and a leather jacket. I think he was the only one to ever pull that off. I told him that once on Facebook. He wasn't too happy about it … I mean, he did pull it off. It was 1985, after all.

Donna: I think Mick Jagger rocked the sweatpants and leather look? [Photo of Mick Jagger and Rolling Stones, Mick Jagger performing live/gettyimages.com.au]

Brian: Ahaha omg that's awesome. They should have a "who wore it better." But my money's on Hooky man. If you ever get nine and a half minutes you gotta watch that video. It is so absurdly awesome. I think Jonathan Demme directed it too.

Donna: Also, Riri wins for sweatpants & leather jacket 500 percent! This is from a few days ago. [Image: Rihanna Wears Her Cult Sweatpants With Heels, Of Course/www.vogue.com]

Brian: I stand corrected.

*

Charles: I was thinking about what makes a breakup album as opposed to someone just writing about failed relationships … I think part of the allure of a breakup album is that you feel that the character who you're interested in, the musician whose record it is, has been pulled into this orbit and is having to do this kind of one-time exorcism.

I used to manage a musician named Bill Morrissey, and Bill Morrissey did a record called *Standing Eight*, and that was about the end of his marriage. A standing eight count in boxing is someone who is still on their feet, but the referee will call the match because he's knocked out, but he's still on his feet … About two-thirds of the songs on the album are specifically about the marriage going south, and they are so excruciatingly open-veined. There's a song called "Last Day of the Last Furlough," which is a line from Salinger, and the refrain of that song is the protagonist, the Bill Morrissey character, with a new girlfriend out on a beach at the end of the day of being out by the water and the refrain is "she wants to make love, I want to drink, drinking is what I do best." And it's, it's just, it's a devastating song …

Donna: How does it feel for them to perform these songs over and over and over again? How do they do that? Do they just disassociate from it, or does it mess them up: what does it do to a person?

Charles: That reminds me of an interview that I read with Jon Dee Graham, the Texas singer-songwriter, who said he and James McMurtry were on tour, and they were both expressing admiration of each other's music, and Jon Dee said to James, "You know, how you are able to create these characters that aren't you and sing about them? I would love to be able to do that." And McMurtry said to him, "I'd love to be able to write like you, but on the other hand, I wouldn't want to bleed out on stage every night."

I can say in Bill Morrissey's case, the songs were such a construction, they were stunningly honest and open veined—but they were still very carefully built, and so I think if you can view something as a piece of art, you can perform it again and again. What I read about Cat Power, of one song going into another and stuff kind of abruptly ending, it sounds like they're less set pieces and more like a stream of consciousness, so it might actually be harder because you don't have that remove of, "I have built this structure into which I'm putting my pain," that would allow you to place the deeply personal song on a shelf as something you can take down and play, as opposed to "I'm living the pain over and over and over again … here's my viscera."

Donna: *Shoot Out the Lights*! How did you learn that was a breakup album?

Charles: In folk-rock circles, Richard and Linda Thompson were so revered. Linda Peters had been a respected folk singer, and she'd married Richard Thompson after he left Fairport Convention, and if you were looking for that particular flavor, it was the ultimate distillation of that particular electric British folk-rock. My college roommate was not into that particular thing, but he liked their music, and when I said I was going to go see Richard Thompson at the Bottom Line in New York, he and his girlfriend came along.

When we got there, he was like, "Where's Linda?" and that hadn't even occurred to me because I was really into the Richard Thompson electric guitar stuff. It was just before *Shoot Out the Lights* came out, and so the people who loved Richard and Linda Thompson were like, "oh, things can't be good in Richard and Linda land." Then the record came out, and the cover of it is Richard Thompson sitting in this kind of demolished room with a bare light bulb swinging back and forth and a photograph of Linda on the wall: "Oh, things are not good, because they couldn't even do a photoshoot of the two of them together." If you're doing a record by a couple and only one of them is in the photo shoot, it's probably a tip-off that things are not going great … if you're listening to the lyric content, there's no mistaking, he does a song, and then she does a song, and if his song is "Don't Renege on Our Love," and her song is "Did She Jump or Was She Pushed" that also kind of sets it off.

Donna: Is it just marketing? Is all of this just a giant marketing scheme that someone somewhere was like, "Oh, you know, these two people were together, and now they're not … "

Charles: Well, I think that's always an aspect. None of the people who we're talking about get to be people we are talking about by being complete shrinking violets. I mean, you take someone like Nick Drake; he was famously averse to public performance. For his album release at the Troubadour in Los Angeles, they got a cardboard cutout of him and played the record with the cardboard cutout sitting on the stage. Smart, smart marketing, and he had to agree to that, you know what I mean? He did kill himself shortly after, but yeah, nobody's perfect.

Author's Top Ten (Probably) Breakup Albums

10. Quasi, *Field Studies*, (1999)
9. Beck, *Sea Change*, (2002)
8. Bob Dylan, *Blood on the Tracks*, (1975)
7. Carole King, *Tapestry*, (1971)
6. Shannon and the Clams, *Gone by the Dawn*, (2015)
5. Cat Power, *Moon Pix*, (1998)
4. Leonard Cohen, *Songs of Love and Hate*, (1971)
3. Smog, *Knock Knock*, (1999)
2. Smog, *The Doctor Came at Dawn*, (1996)
1. Nick Cave & the Bad Seeds, *The Boatman's Call*, (1997)

6

Back of Your Head

Pieces of Reviews from 1998

There's something irresistible about that Chan Marshall, or as I like to call her, the Mark Eitzel of Atlanta. Recording under the Cat Power moniker, she's got a magic coolness that only certain guitar-totin' girls come equipped with ....The record spins through 11 tracks of soft strumming and brittle vocals, all while you rest your head on your pillow, watching a muted black-and-white television, and drifting in and out of consciousness. Not that Moon Pix *makes great sleeping music. Quite the contrary, actually—it's way too interesting.*

Rating: 7.4

Ryan Schreiber, Pitchfork

… It's hard to concentrate on a Cat Power album straight through. Not so much because it's sonically morbid—that's the part I like. But the somber flatness, the

mostly-monochrome which means to make meaning, can get too much … it's supposed to mesmerize and haunt. But if you stare too long it can start to seem vacant.

You're not supposed to stare. That's the whole secret of Cat Power … Chan Marshall writes these terrifically intimate songs, sometimes disturbingly so, but she's not putting on the damage, not doing display. Her songs assume you're looking the other way.

Jane Dark, The Village Voice

… a dazzling line between Sonic Youth and Hank Williams. On this, her fourth album, she sounds like the oldest person alive …

The most affecting moments are saved for "Colors And The Kids," which is quietly suicidal, remembering the best and worst of times. Yet she hangs in there, and the song ends up anthem-like. Her roots in the American South are revealed in "You May Know Him," which is more Otis Redding than Polly Harvey … compared to the latter many times, Moonpix makes this less relevant than ever.

It's no sea of tranquillity, but these lunar landscapes are spectacular enough.

Stuart Bailey, NME

[Chan Marshall] recently told the NME that Moon Pix was the result of her being chased by demons. Bizarrely, then, it doesn't sound violent or terrifying but is definitely other-worldly. Marshall's voice seems to come from some other dimension, it hangs and it haunts, inhabiting an oft sparse

terrain of faintly country-ish hue. Odd but well worth investigating. The Americans might file it under alt. folk.

4 stars

Jonathan Trew, The List, Issue 343

… [Dirty Three's] expressionist soundscapes are a brilliant backdrop for Marshall's dry, breathy voice. The songs slide along at a slow crawl. If you don't slow down your personal timescale and stop what you're doing, the album might just creep away without your noticing it, like the moon disappearing from sight on a cloudy evening. Give it the attention it deserves, and it will reward you with the stunning atmospherics of "Say," complemented with sounds of thunder that were integrated so subtly you might have thought it was actually storming outside …

A.S. Van Dorston, Fast 'n' Bulbous

At least Chan Marshall's not trying to fool anybody. From "she plays the difficult parts and I play difficult" to "the music is boring me to death," she's an honest heroine of the new indie staple—not noise-tune and certainly not irony, both as passe as the guilty pop dreams they kept at bay, but sadness. Slow sadness. Slow sadness about one's inability to relate. And not just to audiences. Hell is other people.

C PLUS

Robert Christgau, The Village Voice

Before Cat Power's fourth full-length, Moon Pix (Matador), came out in September, lead Cat Chan Marshall's genius appeared only in momentary flashes. Don't get me wrong—last year's What Would the Community Think *was a damn fine record. But* Moon Pix *is the record Marshall's admirers knew she had in her. It's a full realization of all her talents …* Moon Pix *breathes fresh air in the wide-open space that characterizes the [Dirty] Three's work. But what makes this album so dazzling is the focus of Marshall's melancholic songwriting and her gripping vocals that flutter, whisper and even howl …*

Gail O'Hara, Time Out New York

From a Conversation with Gail O'Hara, Cofounder of the zine *chickfactor*, Music Editor of *Time Out New York* (1996–2000)

I grew up as this huge fan of music and really wanted to work in entertainment and the arts. I just didn't know how I would fit into that. I never applied myself to learning instruments or had any great dreams of being on stage, except doing karaoke, maybe. In college, I worked as the arts editor at my paper—I learned how to make a fanzine doing that. I really liked it—writing and photography were big things for me at that time. Then I started my career at the *Washington City Paper*, where I had various admin jobs, but I also became a contributing writer, and I had a column on local music.

I moved to New York in February of '92, and I got a job at *Spin* a couple months later. I was the copy chief at *Spin* magazine for three years until I went to *Time Out New York* in '95. I wrote some stuff for *Spin*, but I mostly wasn't taken seriously as a writer or as an editor who could do anything creative. I was told, "You don't have the right sensibility." I had done an interview over the summer of '92 with the guy from the Wedding Present, David Gedge, and *Spin* ended up only using like a quote or two. My friend Pam [Berry] and I decided to start a zine just to run the interview.

I had just moved to New York, and she was my best friend in DC. I would go back to DC, we would work on [our zine] *chickfactor*, and then I would go back to New York. We started working on Macs probably at the beginning of *chickfactor*, and I remember helping Pam learn how to use QuarkXpress (precursor to InDesign) over the phone on our first issue … There's a picture of Phoebe Summersquash on the cover of the first issue, and you can hardly tell who it is because the photo wasn't scanned properly! We probably printed our early issues at Kinko's. We would bring home boxes of paper to my apartment, and we would lie all the pages down on the futon and physically collate them, staple them. Occasionally I would flip through and be like, "somebody put this page in upside down." It was hilarious. Later we started working with a printer in Michigan called D'Printer. They're literally still going, they did our last two issues [*chickfactor* 17, 2012 & *chickfactor* 18, 2018], and they're awesome …

Those years while I was working at *Spin* were probably the most prolific years of *chickfactor* because after I became the music editor at *Time Out New York* it was a lot harder for me to put out more than one issue a year. The freedom of publishing whatever I wanted was a very freeing experience

… [At *Time Out New York*], my relationship with music changed, and I became overwhelmed by how much music I had to deal with. I just quit in 2000 because music was becoming too much work and not what I wanted it to be. It was really hard to say goodbye to all those free tickets and CDs and everything.

*

I worked at *Time Out New York* when it started in September '95. In January of '96, we did an issue called "The Class of '96," and Jonathan Fire*Eater was on the cover?

The bands I wrote about in that feature were Cat Power and Versus. One of the editors there used to joke that when I chose someone to watch, they would actually blow up three years later, not one, not right away. So I wrote about Cat Power. She didn't have any press stuff; Matador's office was right next door to *Time Out* then, so Gerard [Cosloy of Matador] gave us a picture that he took. [Chan] was not a seasoned professional musician at this point, she was young and unsure of herself, and she had this habit of saying "I'm sorry" a lot. She was very sweet. I went to see her whenever I had the chance. I remember seeing her early on at CB's Gallery, and she played with her back to the audience. She just wasn't comfortable as a performer then or comfortable with her own identity yet. I wrote about her in that issue, and then a few months later, I became the music editor at *Time Out New York*, where I was for four years, four and a half years or something. After that feature, we got a complaint letter that's five paragraphs long, and basically this reader was moved to comment about this feature because of Cat Power's inclusion, they said:

> Your 'Class of '96' feature in Issue No. 18 was, for me, of particular interest, having recently moved to New York City and being especially curious and excited about a new music scene. But as I was happily perusing, I came across waify Chan Marshall, a.k.a. Cat Power. My roommate and I attended last year's Liz Phair show at Town Hall and therefore were both subjected to Ms. Marshall. Now, lest we sound like two closed-minded Hootie-ettes

like Hootie and the Blowfish

> please know that Cat Power was, to us, probably the worst live performance we had witnessed in our 46 combined years. That includes amateur piano recitals, impromptu open mike nights, and drunken fraternity karaoke parties.

Imagine being so inspired to write this! This was in the age of faxing in your letter; hardly anyone had e-mail.

> In fact, it was embarrassingly horrendous …She half-warbled, half-whispered, against a spattering of hesitant plucking at her guitar strings …she simply could not play or sing and she knew it. That is why your feature on Miss Marshall is so appalling. Maybe I'm not familiar with the hip lingo that pop music writers employ but to say that a woman who stood shoulders hunched, voice cracking, stopping mid-chord to weep quietly has a 'chilling onstage aura' seems a bit of a stretch. I guess 'from-the-gut and world-weary' are today's polite ways of expressing 'dreadful.' And I guess this type of ridiculous

image-conscious journalism is what rockets talentless bands to stardom.

Obviously, GO,

that's me

whoever he/she is, is sleeping with this particular 'disheveled East Village fox,' because only really, really great sex could make someone lie so very, very well.

That's hilarious, right? It's typed with her address at the end and everything. I don't think we printed it …

I got other letters from people. I wrote about Edith Frost and then got this angry phone voicemail from somebody who went to see her based on my preview and didn't enjoy it … *Time Out New York* also got a letter to the editor from someone about how I was friends with people at Matador, basically accusing me of giving Matador too much coverage and he counted up everything in the issue that was on Matador. I was like, "Well, we kind of review all the music in New York and beyond … you can't really ignore Yo La Tengo and Pavement!"

… But reading that letter back and thinking about my own career trajectory, I feel like we just weren't taken seriously. Women weren't taken seriously at that time. People were shitty to women.

I also did a Cat Power interview for *chickfactor*. We talked about the word *crazy* and how boys, men, characterize women as crazy or hysterical. It's interesting how women have been painted that way. She's such a big talent, and even back then, everybody around could see it—well, not everybody, not that person on the Upper East Side who wrote that letter. She was such a talent, and certain people she played music with, like Steve Shelley or the Dirty Three guys, would kind of ground her in that moment and help her focus. Another thing we talked about in *chickfactor* was how she wanted to leave New York. The interview took place in the summer of '96, but she was like, "I want to leave New York because I can't concentrate here," and I thought it was interesting that she needed to find focus and evolve slowly. Chan was normal. She was insecure, and that's normal. She was uncomfortable as a performer, and that's normal, she was inconsistent, and that's normal. Not everybody is gonna be perfect every day at whatever they do.

*

This was just on the very cusp of the change from actually having an underground to going on to the internet world. People had more time to develop their careers, and *Time Out* was part of the reason that the underground died, along with the internet, because ultimately that's where it all went. People used to spend years playing shows before everyone knew who they were … the internet wasn't documenting things the way they were later. Someone like Amy Winehouse would have complete meltdowns on stage, and it was all on YouTube the next day, and that's kind of what killed her … In a way, we're lucky that YouTube wasn't around in 1996. Musicians are human. They're flawed. And anybody who's seen a good Cat Power show knows that it's amazing, and not everyone's going to get what she's doing.

7

Moonshiner

A Statement

The idea of doing a cover song today is usually about novelty or some marketing gimmick. But actually interpreting songs— that's part of the thread work of the history of music. It's tradition … it's the same shit that we've been doing since people first started making songs, whether it be country or jazz or whatever. Everybody has always sung everybody else's songs. It's about the song … So I hate it when people complain about me doing so many covers. It's part of a tradition. It's a part of the craft.

*Chan Marshall interviewed by
T. Cole Rachel,* Interview, *2012*

*

1998
"Moonshiner" (recorded: Melbourne, Australia)
Chan Marshall (born: Georgia)

"Moonshiner" is a slow dirge: stark, bleak and crawling, "You're already in hell, You're already in hell, I wish we could go to hell," Chan howls, maybe referencing her waking nightmare in South Carolina. "Holy, holy," describes a whiskey still and a dewy vine, evoking two different kinds of spirits. Marshall speaks of "handsome men" with skeptical longing and regret. The final word is Marshall's own, "life ain't worth the drown," followed by straggling, strummed chords as the song falls apart, floating in the weight and weightlessness of the drink. The first version of the song Marshall heard was Dylan's, as written in *Pitchfork*:

> *I was in a lover's bedroom, and the* Bootleg Series *had just come out. I hadn't gotten it yet, and he played it. I was so in love with this person who was so abusive. I just came to terms with it recently. He was a good man, he just had a lot of demons. He put this on, and it validated my pain, and listening somehow took the pain away. "Moonshiner" was the softest bed I could ever lie on. I felt validated,* **realized**.

The back of the *Moon Pix* album features a small photo of Dylan, a shot taken of a television set while he plays mid-song.

*

1991 (Released)
"Moonshiner" or "Moonshine Blues" (r.1963, NYC)
Bob Dylan (b. Minnesota)

Classic Dylan on guitar, harmonica, and vocals. His extended harmonica solos—the notes he holds just a hair too long—

drag you along to his next lyric, where he always does the real work. It's an outtake from *The Times They Are a Changing*, not released until the *Bootleg Series 1-3* in the early '90s. Like all of Dylan's writing, his subtle word shifts feel deliberate, hinting at a sense of a larger inequality he wants his spotlight to share.

Carla Rotolo, the sister of Dylan's girlfriend Suzy (most famously joining him on the cover of *The Freewheelin' Bob Dylan*), was the assistant to ethnomusicologist Alan Lomax which is where Dylan could have first heard the song. Or maybe he heard it in the Greenwich Village clubs where the song also thrived. Suzy, in her autobiography *A Freewheelin' Time*, said this about the scene and their obsession with covers:

> Back in those days, the study of the origins of traditional music was a passion among musicians. Some folksingers believed they had to perform songs authentically in the traditional style with no deviation from the way the original singer sang it on the scratchy old LPs they listened to ... A folksinger who dared reinterpret a traditional song by adding a personal inflection of some sort was scorned as inauthentic. Yet most of these performers were about as authentic as Las Vegas. They were middle-class city or suburban kids who had never been near a backwoods except at summer camp.

Yet personal flourishes might be what allows a cover to endure.

*

1972

"I Wish I was a Moonshiner" or "Moonshiner" (r. California
as Virginia on The Waltons)
Jason Walton (John Walmsley, b. England) featuring
Yancy Tucker (Robert Donner, b. NYC)

The Waltons was an American TV show about the title family
set in their fictional town in Virginia's Blue Ridge Mountains via
the Warner Bros. studio lot and Hollywood Hills. Thirteen years
in nine seasons, the show began with the Great Depression and
ended with the Second World War. In Season Seven, Episode
9, there is a subplot about making moonshine so pure it could
power a car. At one point, Jason Walton, also a musician in real
life, shows up to sing to the men working on the still, delivering
his ballad propped oddly against a log on the fake ground. The
All About the Waltons FaceBook page notes:

> There is debate as to the origin of the tune and lyrics but
> it is interesting to note that country music star Tex Ritter
> recorded a song he titled "Rye Whiskey" in 1933 based on
> the song "Jack of Diamonds" which is said to have roots to
> "Rye Whiskey" Tex Ritter of course is the father of John
> Ritter who played Reverend Fordwick on The Waltons.

The page also tracks "Jack of Diamonds" back to Blind
Lemon Jefferson's 1926 version of the song, its melody a faint
hum of the future "Moonshiner."

*

1964
"Kentucky Moonshiner" (r. 1962, New York?)
Dave Van Ronk (b. New York)

"Moonshiner" appears on *Inside Dave Van Ronk*, strummed chords supporting his bellowing voice. He sings with an inflection that emphasizes syllables, growing crescendos peak and recede, a measured delivery that gives the sense that a whole other instrument is present: the guitar, the vocalist saying words, the sounds that hover around outside those words. The '60s Greenwich Village folk scene set a scaffold for future city music scenes to thrive: coffeeshops/clubs, record stores, political discourse, tiny apartments where lives were lived, and music shared. Clubs like Gerdes, the Bitter End, the Figaro, and Fat Black Pussy Cat, padded the streets. Dave Van Ronk was a folk scene mainstay, nicknamed the "Mayor of MacDougal St." He would cycle out crowds at the famous Gaslight, sending voyeurs on their way to replace them with more for maximum profit. His dense knowledge of music & political history crafted cerebral, blues-influenced renditions and calculated folk covers. The 2013 film by the Coen Brothers, *Inside Llewelyn Davis*, is an impression based on Van Ronk's autobiography published after his death in 2003. The film premiered at the Cannes Film Festival and won the Grand Prix.

*

1965
"Moonshiners" (r. New York)
Barbara Müller (b. Tennessee) & Wendy Caesar (b.?)

Rich harmonies of two women's voices call out with a forlorn, beckoning fullness, like psych Rock/Jefferson Airplane. Maybe it's the long notes held, ending with a vibrato? Or the mildly unsettling harmonies? Crooning '50s rock also rises with its sincerity, enunciation, and crisp guitar that eventually adds rhythm to the disembodied vocals. The song is found on *Double Premiere* put out on Quote Records in 1965, introducing Tennessee-born Müller and also the songwriter showcased on the album, Canadian Sonia Brock. The label's liner notes hold the most info on the mysterious Müller's lone album: *"One night while attending the Hootenanny at the Greenwich Village Bitter End, we took down the name Barbara Müller—a tall green-eyed blonde with a candid style and exceptionally pure voice."* It was Müller's first time in New York, urged to go by the folk club engineer at the Music Conservatory of Oberlin College in Ohio. Barbara Müller now teaches in the Philosophy and Religion Departments at a University. She performs in Floridian Folk Festivals, introduced at one show with the following: *"Let's welcome another Super Star. Of course, you don't have stars at folk festivals, do you? But you do have people you enjoy hearing, and we have so many. Barbara Müller from Lake Mary!"*

*

1960s
"Moonshiner" (live)
Karen Dalton (b. Texas)

Dalton was never able to make it huge, even though she shared stages with Dylan, the Holy Modal Rounders, and is often cited as an influence to generations of musicians that followed. The reasons for her lack of traditional success may have been the booze and drugs that haunted her, or her tumultuous relationships (one resulting in missing teeth). The artifacts of her existence, beyond her recordings, include a film of her casually trotting on a horse, grainy photos of her face in mid-song, a music video from the early days of music videos where novelty superseded aesthetics. In the 2020 documentary *In My Own Time: A Portrait of Karen Dalton*, ephemera left behind from her death in 1993 lingers. Poems, letters, set lists, her life condensed into forgotten boxes, all of which perished in a fire soon after the documentary finished shooting. This movie is now the only record of those memories. Scribbled across some images of setlists, the faint title "Moonshiner" can be seen. Imagine an acoustic guitar floating behind her incomparable voice, a rough texture baying into the moody clubs or into the thickness of a forest, places where she felt most at home. Her voice dry, cracked, spectral, reaching out from another, unknown dimension, from an altered state of being.

*

1959
"Kentucky Moonshiner" (r. California)
Rolf Cahn (b. Germany)

"Kentucky Moonshiner" is sped up, a super-fast, classical guitar sound, weightless and flying. Vocals are a lone male, a tight vibrato (think Robbie Basho). Rolf Cahn's family escaped Germany on the cusp of the Second World War, landing in Detroit, Michigan. He eventually settled in San Francisco on the cusp of the folk revival. He founded the club Blind Lemon in the '50s and then helped run The Cabale (also called The Cabale Creamery for reasons unknown), both vital clubs in the Berkeley scene hosting acts like Odetta and Larry Moore in their San Pablo Avenue locations. When the folk scene ebbed, Cahn dedicated himself to martial arts writing the book *K'ang Jo Fu: Self Defense for Gentle People*.

*

1959
"The Moonshiner" (r. NYC)
The Clancy Brothers & Tommy Makem (b. Ireland)

A slow ballad, a harmonica, and a mournful male voice, a collaged mix of lyrics and sounds with origins ranging (supposedly) from a seventeenth-century Scottish ballad and traditional Irish folk music. It appears on the album *Come Fill Your Glass with Us: Irish Songs of Drinking & Blackguarding*: alcohol is predominant. "O moonshine dear moonshine o how I love thee, you killed my poor father but dare you try me," grieves the vocalist. A later version by The Clancy Brothers, Makem & Pete Seeger is the opposite of this; a spirited, drinking song with hoots, hollers, yips, and yays, a collective chorus, a celebration. Imagine them rowdy and precise, clad in their signature cable-knit sweaters, gently sweating, and full of drink toasting to an audience in a New York Club, out of place but manifesting the scene to be their own.

*

1951
"The Moonshiner" (r. London, Dublin or New York)
Delia Murphy (b. Ireland)

Murphy's accordion and her single voice, strong with a mild warble, includes a nod to her fellow female sots: "I'll have moonshine for Liza and moonshine for May, moonshine for Lou, and she'll sing all the day." It's lighter, downy, positive but with some undertone of secrets. Delia Murphy, aka The Queen of Connemara (a coastal town in Western Ireland), was supposedly singing this song since the '30s. Murphy was a collector of Irish folk ballads, a hobby that was helpful after marrying a man who became an Irish diplomat & ambassador, singing at parties, raising four children, and balancing her impressive singing career.

*

1949
"Moonshiner" (r. New York)
Mickey & Mary Carton (b. New York)

A waltz-like fiddle, flute, and accordion (Mickey Carton) with a jaunty female vocalist (Mary Carton) that feels like a carousel ride. The brother and sister duo hailed from the Bronx, taking up their traditional Irish folk roots and making them Irish-American. They were well known in the Rockaways, a beach peninsula in Queens that welcomed crowds at clubs like the Dublin House. Mickey was an electrician who served in the Second World War and spent his nights as a bandleader, a performer with skill and charisma that earned him the nickname "Mr. Rockaway," appearances on the Ed Sullivan Show, and a street named after him upon his death in 1992, "Mickey Carton Way." There is a mention of Mickey performing as part of Kennedy's 1961 Presidential Inaugural Ball, but he might have been a performer as part of the Pre-Inaugural event hosted by Frank Sinatra, a huge star-studded gala/fundraiser to pull the Democratic campaign out of debt.

*

1937
"The Moonshiner" (r. Kentucky)
Daw/Daugh/Dawson Henson (b. Kentucky)

Dawson plays fast on the guitar. His vocal melody feels like a boulder thrown out into the air only to rapidly descend, a repeated gesture with little reprieve. A woman's voice at the recording's end notes the singer, location, and date, like a tag on an artifact. The end of Dawson's recording has some tuning and guitar sounds, a sense of life beyond the recording. As Suze Rotolo notes in her autobiography, " ... *the Lomax field recordings and Harry Smith's Anthology of American Folk Music delivered this music from back porches and local communities out into the world at large. They gave us an invaluable legacy: a musical heritage.*" Alan and his wife Elizabeth drove on dirt, stopping to strike up conversations with locals to hunt down music, rarities because they were isolated high in the mountains, untouched by time. The fading coal towns hid the fading music, and Lomax feverishly worked to make sure the sounds were not lost, solidifying their place in history. The recording equipment used was a portable direct-to-disc machine, etching onto a lacquered disc of glass or aluminum between 6 and 16 inches in diameter—the highly fragile records did not take kindly to the rugged Appalachian roads. The equipment weighed a few hundred pounds, the battery died often, and needles wore down fast. On this particular trip to Kentucky, Elizabeth was mostly ill, which left Alan and a handler to lug the recorder into homes, or record out of the trunk of their car.

*

1937
"The Moonshiner Song" (r. Kentucky)
Kenneth Begley (b. Kentucky)

Hell for Certain in Leslie County, Kentucky, is where Kenneth Begley was recorded, a sparse, eerie vocal rendition. His voice filled the room: a strange sound of rhythm—maybe a hand on the knee or a foot on the floor—keeping a loose beat for his wails that hedge on a yodel. Begley's voice turned this way and that without notice. The static almost gets in the way of the music, the lyrics solitary but contented: "No woman to follow to see what I spend. No children to squeal and squall if you want to live happy, don't marry at all." Sounds that echo the Great Depression, living a life full of emotional and financial loneliness and loss; the only thing to be counted on was the bottle. Lomax's view of his role in collecting folk songs changed dramatically throughout his life. In John Szwed's book *Alan Lomax: The Man Who Recorded the World*, he speaks plainly about how Lomax first viewed his role as a collector. He saw himself as a cataloguer trying to amass words and titles of found music, but, later on, he realized it was the performances—the people behind the performances—that truly represented something, as Szwed notes: "Folklore could show what it meant to be an American."

*

1927
"Old Whisker Bill, The Moonshiner" (r. New York)
Buell Kazee (b. Kentucky)

A quick banjo gallops, set against a soft-sounding bed of vocals recorded deep into prohibition. His voice is forthright but with some sense of hesitancy, as if he is slowly divulging a secret. Buell Kazee was pulled from Burton Fork, Kentucky into a NY studio by the owner of a phonograph shop in

Ashland, Kentucky. Kazee became a preacher for over twenty years as the Great Depression put his music on hold. The '60s folk revival brought him and his banjo back to life, even though he is said to have considered music just a hobby. According to legend, Kazee first came across a homemade banjo at his Aunt's house when he was five years old, as noted in the *Kentucky Baptist Heritage* newsletter, *"The instrument was a whittled piece of walnut, the hoop was made from split white oak, and a home-tanned cat skin hide was stretched over the hoop and fastened with carpet tacks."* Kazee died in 1976, America's bicentennial, at the age of seventy-six.

8

You May Know Him

Touring

Thirty to forty shows and radio appearances began in September 1998, right after the release of *Moon Pix*, and ended in the tip of November. The tour snaked through the US looping from New York, down the East Coast, into the South, across Texas, up the West Coast and then into the Midwest, Canada and through the top of New England, back into New York. Mick Turner joined the tour in California, possibly replacing Mark Moore on guitar. Each night they would most likely descend into clubs, emerge on stage, then, after the show, roll into a strange bed where cigarettes were still welcome and landlines gave some sense of connection.

A Show in the United States

September 28 or 29, 1998—Athens, Georgia, 40 Watt Club

Line Up: Chan Marshall, Mark Moore & Jim White

Set List: "Metal Heart," "Dreams/Weighted Down," "He Turns Down," "Naked, If I Want To," "American Flag," "Werewolf," "Cross Bones Style," "Leopard and the Lamb," "Colors and the Kids"

A brick building hugs the corner of the downtown, tree-lined street in Athens, Georgia. A marquee announces Cat Power. The windows are blacked out, keeping out the remnants of the day and keeping eyes from looking in. Christmas lights are strung from the rafters; their dim efforts provide a nostalgic comfort and a way to hide dirt, spilled drinks, or other mistakes. The bar glows red, the long counter stretches across, bartenders cover the expanse like goalies. A small, lone disco ball shimmers in the middle of the floor.

A person with an early camcorder hovers in the crowd, a backseat cinematographer directs the director, "She doesn't look this way ever … she always looks off to the side," he wants to be helpful. Years later words would be coined to explain this phenomenon, perfected by male '90s music nerd: mansplaining.

Chan stands to the right, her hair covering her face, her body behind her black and white Silvertone guitar. The stage seems too small. Her white button-down shirt is unbuttoned slightly, revealing a thin gold chain around her neck, her cuffs are undone, flapping over her wrists, black rubber bracelets connect hand to arm. Her blue jeans are miss-shapen; the outline of wallets past are worn into the back pockets. Mark, the guitarist, looks like the image of a guitarist: austere, posturing, a necklace hanging loosely. He noodles on his guitar, loud and menacing. Chan's painted toenails peek out from flip flops.

Jim White, the drummer, doesn't fit in. He wears a suit jacket. His brushes and sticks whirr through the air. It's hard to tell when exactly they make contact. He can break a beat down into 1,000 moments, landing anywhere on the spectrum with exactitude. Someone once said, "You either get three musicians or one Jim White." It's a hometown crowd for Mark and Chan, so there are familiar faces and expectations.

Mark approaches Chan; it's hard to tell what he's trying to communicate. It seems like a mix of brotherly love and band dynamics. She whispers into the mic, *"What is the next song?"* Mark touches her elbow to tell her something, which she seems to instantly echo, *"Matt Sweeney is here … I thought Smoke was supposed to be here … mix up,"* speaking of her good friend Benjamin, the throaty howling poet whose queer Southern Gothic poured like honey onto gravel. *"It's not me. I am pretending,"* the lyrics of "He Turns Down" ring out.

Chan enters a trance-like state, repeating a musical theme. She seems like she's waiting until she feels ready to sing. The guitarist and drummer's eyes flit toward her for a signal. After a compact version of "Cross Bones Style" ends, she speaks: *"Ooo, confidence, yeah."*

The person filming the show zooms in on things: the drum kit, a microphone, a hand. They also switch up the limited filters available: sepia, negative, black & white, color.

"This next song is another cover song," Chan removes ownership, maybe to feel more at peace, more comfortable, *"I apologize it's not enough."* When the song ends, she starts to play, heading into another trance of solace. The guitarist grabs her arm, gently nudging in an "it's time to stop" gesture. She looks embarrassed like she isn't following the unwritten

rules, possibly a reminder of her musician father, shooing her away from the sanctity of instruments. She isn't following the definition of a rock star. Is she rejecting the imitation of an imitation?

She briskly swigs some bottled water, closes it, and begins to roll up her cables and pack up her gear. The club's volume goes up, a raucous pop song pounding its fists into the air creeps in, obliterating the stillness hanging from the show.

The cameraperson focuses on the disco ball.

*

Television performances or interviews were very rare but still existed. Usually, some sort of host would be present and ask questions or announce performers. It was another type of performance with a different set of challenges.

A Televised Interview in Canada on The Wedge

October 26, 1998 (dates disputed, may have aired in 1999)

A woman with a large microphone, Sook-Yin Lee, sits off-screen, Chan sits in front of a camera. The background is odd, like a dirty basement: an unmoving lava lamp, some black trash bags, ugly desks, a styrofoam cup. The large microphone dips on-screen once Chan is prompted to answer. The questions are incredibly thoughtful, better than usual.

"Do you consider yourself a spiritual person? Because this album is a little more spiritual," asks the disembodied voice about *Moon Pix*.

"*Spiritual, I think is normal, it's a normal warmth and communication that we don't really know how to speak, but I think we all share it. In my music? Is that what you asked? I don't know, I hope it is, but I think everyone hopes that an aspect of what they do in their life has something that is something good,*" replies Chan.

The video is edited with awkward overlays and fades; there's even a green screen cutout of Chan performing in the "Cross Bones Style" music video. There is also a peculiar '90s editing decision of threepeating a quick phrase like a misplaced shock jock aesthetic, "You know what I mean/You know what I mean/You know what I mean?" The segment ends with Chan shaking her hair in slow motion. Another unnatural movement stuck in time.

*

November and December brought Cat Power to Europe, where the fan base was growing. Chan did another thirty to forty shows and radio performances, at times moving from opener to headliner as her popularity grew. The band moved through the UK, Germany, Switzerland, France, Spain, and then the Netherlands. Mark Moore played with her, Jim played some of the shows replaced with a drummer (possibly Chris Lopez) after the UK. She viewed touring as a part of the job and she needed the job to pay the bills. She wrote sixty postcards on this tour to friends, lovers, family to help stay connected. At night she would work out cover songs in her hotel rooms, inching toward her next album.

A Show in Europe

November 26, 1998—Bern, Switzerland, ISC Club Bern

Lineup: Chan Marshall, Christopher Lopez (?), Mark Moore

Set List: "Moonshiner," "Say," "He Was A Friend of Mine," "American Flag," "Metal Heart," "Cross Bones Style," "Leopard and the Lamb," "Dreams," "Naked, If I Want To," "He Turns Down," "Rockets," "King Rides By," "Back of Your Head," "Colors and the Kids," "From Fur City," "You May Know Him," "Sea of Love," "Break, Break, Break Your Back"

What do ya'll think? You think the vocals are too loud out there?"
The crowd responds with yeses and nos.
("He Was a Friend of Mine," "American Flag")

"Wondering if I could get some of my guitar out of these monitors. Are you all sure the vocals aren't really loud and that everything else is real quiet out there? Does it sound loud? Like the other instruments? Do they sound loud out there? Sorry."

After a near-perfect version of "Metal Heart" Chan exclaims, *"Great song!"*
("Cross Bones Style," "Leopard and the Lamb")

" … If it sounds bad, you don't want to do anything, you know what I mean? If it sounds bad, it doesn't encourage you to do anything, you know what I mean?"

("Dreams" A cover of Fleetwood Mac from *Rumours*)

A cut and what seems like an encore.
More *sorrys* and songs.
"Fans. Loving companions. Why'd ya'll stick around?"
"Cause it's great!"
"It is?"
"Yeah!"
"You all are fucking insane … "

*

Radio in Europe

November 23, 1998—München, Germany, Bayerischer Rundfunk (Public Radio)

Lineup: Mark Moore and Chan Marshall

Set List: "He Was a Friend of Mine," "Naked, If I Want To," "Werewolf," "Say," "Metal Heart," "He Turns Down," "Dreams," "I Found A Reason," "Let Sadness Not Be Attached to Your Name"/"Keep On Running," "Colors and the Kids," "From Fur City"

An introduction is made in German. An overproduced, whizzing, whirring, early '90s intro assaults. Mark Moore and Chan sit in a room with instruments, mics, headphones. After the songs, a hollow clapping of the few people in the room slaps out. A creaking chair, the tuning of a guitar, *"I apologize."*

At the end of "Metal Heart," Chan whispers, "Thank You," inhales, and slowly exhales.

After "Dreams," Chan moves over to play solo on the piano, *"Uh, sorry, just gonna get my headphones here and put them on and sit down,"* politely narrating for listeners. The piano seems to create a struggle.

At the end of her piano set, the announcer urges, "Can you go on, Chan?"

"That's it."

"Oh, come on," he says with a minor sneer.

"I couldn't hear the thing at all," she seems agitated.

"Chan, could we talk you into doing one more, two more, songs for us?"

There is no right answer to this question. She says "no," she disappoints, she says "yes," she has to perform in less than ideal conditions.

"Yeah .... Which should I do? I-I-I-I"

The announcer invites Mark back into the room.

Mark tries to step in, maybe soothe her, like a relative or a true friend. He suggests "Colors and the Kids" slow, on the piano. Next, he suggests another song, "You wanna do the Benjamin song?"

"Yeah, do one more for us, and, um, we greatly appreciate you being here tonight … "

German is spoken, Chan can be heard in the background.

Chan growls a bit, *"Dammit. Excuse me, pardon me."*

Mark distracts with a fast guitar lick of "Don't Fear the Reaper." *"I can barely hear my guitar, by the way. Sorry...,"* with resignation, *"Sorry, Germany."*

A flawless "From Fur City," a tribute to Benjamin Smoke, ends.
"I'm completely out of tune, completely," the room claps, *"Thank you very much. I'm sorry."*
More clapping, more German.

*

November 20 or 30, 1998—Paris, France, Planet Claire Radio

> Line Up: On Aligre 93.1 FM Chan appears solo on acoustic guitar.

> Set List: (partial setlist?) "Kingsport Town," "Wild Is the Wind," "Red Apples," "Great Expectations"

"Is it rolling, mate? Okay. Is this live?"
"No."
"Oh fuck."

Her voice is liquid, languid. Her guitar strong and forward. She seems at ease or at least comfortable enough to perform. Before starting "Wild Is the Wind," she tells everyone not to look. They close the door. She admonishes herself for mistakes, *"It sucks 'cause it's supposed to go …"* but there aren't as many "sorrys" or "are you mads," or, if there are, the existing recording has edited them out. Her songs are moving and profound. The French get her. They respect her with her aloof cleverness, her effortless style, her bangs. The world-weariness in Chan's voice takes center stage, her vocals shine. The last song rolls out in a deliberate drone-like chord. It resonates through the mic, through the air, through the airwaves: "*I am the snow, I am the snow, I happen to be the snow.*"

From a Conversation with Jim Romeo, Cofounder of Ground Control Touring and Booker of the US *Moon Pix* Tour

I just was a fan of music, a fan of live music, and I hung around clubs. I met this guy named Bob who was a manager and a booking agent. I just kept on kind of bothering him. I was a big fan of bands he worked with; he could tell that I was kind of serious about it. I tried not to bother him too much, but I remember I would sometimes record shows; I'd be like a bootlegger or whatever with a portable mic. I remember recording one of his bands. He said, "make sure I get a copy of that," and I was like, "Sure."

At the time, I was living in New Jersey, but I was going to school in New York. I went by the office, and I brought the tape by, and it just so happened that he started a new agency two or three months before. They needed an assistant because they had a summer intern that just left. I was working for my stepfather and going to school—I'm not sure what I was going to do, you know? I know I want something with music, in fact, I was going to school for audio engineering in the city, but I wasn't really that into it … I know I want to do something live, and I'm not really sure what it is. I never really thought about that, and then I said, "if you need some help around here, let me know," and then he called a week later.

I was like, "Okay, I can figure this out," and became an assistant and just did mailings and all kinds of paperwork. Eventually, I picked up a band here and there and just kind of went from there.

I was starting to venture out of going to big rock concerts into small clubs, and I remember when I started doing that and going to CBGB's, then places like Maxwell's in Hoboken, which I ended up living above for a while. I just knew I liked that sort of vibe and the bands that passed through there. I was sort of like: "I want to be part of this." Not just be a fanboy, be a little bit more.

I wasn't very musically inclined. I tried to play an instrument … I threw that part aside. I have a big fear of public speaking, and I could not think about going on stage and facing an audience of people. To me, it feels very weird and foreign, and some people are cut out for it, and some are not, you know?

*

It was different pre-internet. I started back in 1990, and we used to literally have a routing calendar—not a calendar, like a sheet—and we'd just write the routing in, you write the phone number, and you call the people up at the club when they would be there—booking hours were 3 to 6 (or whatever) on Tuesdays and Thursdays. So you have to call them, then hold the date … certain aspects of it are still the same as they are now, but it was just a more Luddite approach. Faxing, I guess, was just starting. I don't even know how it happened before that … you would get offers that were faxed to you. Then you'd make a contract and then make an itinerary, but it was a lot of paper. A lot of paper [laughs] was involved, and you gave all that paper to the people before they go on tour … If you lost the paper, then you lost everything. We used to have these tour booklets, which I guess they still make now sometimes. I don't think Chan had a tour manager. I want to say that she had a friend helping out briefly. I think it was just the three [musicians].

*

[*Moon Pix*] was really interesting because all the other stuff was made with people's help, and this was made with the Dirty Three's help, but it seemed like she went to Australia and came back with this record that blew everybody away because it just arrived and it was like "whoa." This record was much different in a sense, more realized and kind of done, kind of away from everything. The previous record, *What Would the Community Think*, was done in Memphis with the guy who produced Pavement, and Steve Shelley was running the show because he had experience with that. The recordings before that were just done in New York at just some cheap studio … really lo-fi stuff. So this was just a really interesting thing. She had the whole concept and just had it done, here it is, "boom," boom like that … there was the whole backstory of how she wrote the songs, that whole thing when she lived in South Carolina. I visited her once there in South Carolina, and, yeah, it was the middle of nowhere, literally the middle of nowhere in this farmhouse with a bunch of land behind it, a very small town in South Carolina. There wasn't much else to do there … She wrote a lot of those songs in that time period, which would have been fall of '97. She really didn't play any shows then … so a lot of those songs people never really heard because she didn't even take them out on the road. So that was sort of the interesting thing about that record because, with all the records before, she was working out the material live, it was kind of done, and with [*Moon Pix*], that one was just like a big birth of an album, it just kinda dropped.

9

Colors and the Kids

A Piece of a Show Review

She forgot lyrics, let the simplest strumming patterns crumble and fall apart, and by the end of her endless set arrived at abject contrition. "It's not cool," she said, berating herself. "It's not funny. I'm sorry." And then she walked off, leaving the crowd in disbelief. Her guitar player strolled to center stage. "Turn the lights on," he instructed. "It's over."
Ben Ratliff, The New York Times, *1999*

Some References to the Show Review

But her bad concerts can be worse than just awkward. They can be public meltdowns akin to bizarre performance art. These occasions are extremely rare, but … they are what people remember. The most infamous show (and Chan's personal worst) was in 1999 at the Bowery Ballroom. In a New York Times review (which Chan says is her favorite article on her because of its honesty) the concert was called "staggering for its inversion of standard rock performance ethics. Gone was the idea of exultation, or of showing what one can do; in its place was outrageously passive-aggressive behavior and non-musicianship."

William Van Meter, NY Magazine, 2006

She hasn't always dealt with her fans' emotional hunger so simply. Her notoriously irregular live shows reached their nadir in a well-documented performance at Manhattan's Bowery Ballroom in 1999. Prostrate and foetal on the floor of the auditorium, she sang the dirge-like Cross Bones Style with her nose pressed into the ground, while fans gathered round her awkwardly, stroking her and murmuring consolations.

Hermione Hoby, The Guardian, 2012

People aren't drawn to her because of one song, or one era: it's her. Certain people may be stupid and selfish for going to Cat Power gigs and hoping for one of her infamous on-stage meltdowns (the release of Moon Pix was overlooked until a real fiasco of a show at New York's Bowery Ballroom in January 1999, where Marshall was so nervous she didn't complete a single song, told the crowd her band hated her, and in the end, collapsed into a ball, sobbing, on stage, only to have her fans get up on stage and pat her on the back).

Nicky Smith, Splice Today, 2012

From a Conversation with Writer Ben Ratliff
on His *New York Times* Show Review

I had never seen anything like that performance before, and I have not seen anything like it since. It short-circuited me within my conception of what a critic does so severely that I really had to think about what my purpose was. I was sure that I would not be satisfied with whatever way I chose to handle it, and, indeed, I'm not satisfied [laughs] with the way I chose to handle it. Okay, well, so let's see, it was 1999.

January 1999, so I was thirty, and I had started writing at *The Times* in '96 after six years of freelancing and working at book publishers and not really knowing what the future was going to hold. But I was sort of following my nose and doing what I wanted to do, on the assumption that at some point, something would break and one path would become clear. I just kept on writing for *The Village Voice* and other places through the 90s, and then finally somebody from *The Times* called me and said, "We need some help. We need another stringer and, especially because you write about jazz, among other things, we can use somebody like you. Are you ready to do that job?" Which was not a salary and not a contract. You just got paid by the piece, but there was plenty of work, and I was so ready to change direction and say, "Yep, I'm going to do that." So it all worked out, and I kept at it, and, finally, I got a job there. By '99, I probably was on staff at *The Times*, or at least—whether I was on contract or staff—I think I felt some measure of security in my job. I felt sort of installed, you know? And I was really happy, I mean it couldn't have been better. It wasn't just that I had the full run of non-classical music to write about—it wasn't just like, "Ah, we don't know what it is you do, just do whatever you want"—they *knew* what I was doing. There was actually a kind of tradition at the paper, or there had been for at least ten, fifteen years, where it was the job of "jazz and pop" critics—that was the technical designation at the paper, "jazz and pop" critics—to write about all kinds of music and to develop a really broad beat. And I was like, damn, this is *exactly* what I want to do. Jazz and Brazilian music and African music and punk and experimental music and hip hop and r&b … in the span of a month you'd be writing about all those things.

*

I knew who Cat Power was. I knew *what* it was. I knew … I don't know whether I had heard the first two records or not, but I was certainly aware of them. I knew the sounds. I wasn't a fan, I wasn't a follower, but I basically knew what she was about. And then *Moon Pix* really impressed me. I mean, it's so special. Was I aware at the time that Chan had a history of weird performances? I'm not sure. How could I not have been, right? But I just can't remember.

I don't know what expectations I had when I went there. But I just remember thinking, these songs are not very complicated; the material is not difficult to pull off. She's got "it," whatever "it" is, so this will be good. And you know … um … It was really hard to watch. I started thinking harder and harder as I watched it: how am I going to write about this? What's the proper way? I remember all the stopping and starting. I remember the sense that it was very, very much like a bad dream, where you can't move forward. You know the kind of dreams where you can't—you're trying to do a very simple action, but you can't do it? It was like watching somebody else in that state in real life. Terrifying, actually. I do remember when she came down from the stage into the audience, and the band kept playing. I don't know whether she had her guitar with her, or a microphone or whatever. I can't remember, did she lie down flat on the floor sort of spread out? Or did she just sit cross-legged and put her ....? But she put her face on the floor, she put her nose on the floor and *stayed* there, and a whole bunch of audience members came around and touched her, and patted her, as if to say, "It's okay. We love you," that kind of gesture. Stroking her, petting her. I know that I sort of pushed into that circle to see what was happening, because something was happening, and I was there to write about it, and so I had to see. I had the weird feeling of, like, I don't know what I'm disturbed by more: the people patting her, or what I was doing, which was to muscle in to watch it. And then ... you know, it ended. And she said the thing: "It isn't funny ....It isn't cool, it isn't funny, I'm sorry." If everything else hadn't been confusing enough, that was like a whole other twist. If you're going to see the mercurial artist, the mercurial artist does not at the end say: "This wasn't cool, it's not funny, I'm sorry." That doesn't happen, you know? Can you imagine Bob Dylan saying that? You know what I mean? It was just totally bewildering. And so then I had a choice.

I had canceled reviews before that. But, generally, the paper would send a photographer to all the shows that I was covering, and so I felt that I didn't want to waste the paper's money by sending a photographer out and not following through with a review. Also, I was young, and I felt some security, but I still kind of needed to be a responsible member of the newsroom—so I wasn't just going to lots of shows and then canceling the review. I would be quite careful about which ones I chose to cancel, and the ones I chose to cancel tended to be, oh, a really dull performance, not a lot of people in the audience and, eh, this thing isn't really important, I might have misjudged the importance of the thing beforehand and so let's just forget that it happened, it's really not that important. But this one was different, because there were a lot of people there, and something *happened*, and the something that happened seemed to have something to do with her work and her art. In my mind, it seemed that maybe it even had something to do with a larger tradition that was being built at the time of these kinds of singer-songwriters. So I left, and I remember walking a very long distance just trying to figure it out; I couldn't just go home.

It was just a really tricky moment like, fuck, what do I do? I ended up writing this review, which I read it over just the other day, and it seems to be … a bit chiding, a bit … reprimanding, you know? My position, the position that I felt that I wanted to occupy, was "look: I'm not one of your fans; it doesn't matter whether I'm your fan or not. I'm not one of the people patting you. I'm not part of an inner circle. I'm not protecting anything here. I'm an interested critic. I'm an insider/outsider," you know? I felt that the only way to do it was to maintain some degree of objectivity, and I know that

that whole concept is … to be doubted. But I just felt really strongly here that if there can be some kind of objectivity, I can cling to that, and that's the way I'm going to do it.

The main question for me now is, what would I have done now? I don't know whether the right thing to do would have been to cancel the review or to write the review in the driest way possible. If there were a way to do it—okay, let me just change course for a second. What I didn't know then, about what I could do in writing a critical review for the *New York Times*, was: I could have written about the difficulty I was having writing about it. I could have made that explicit, and I could have worked that into the review in a concise way that wouldn't be laying my own problems on the reader. It's possible. People do it now. Like, for instance, Parul Sehgal, who writes book reviews for *The Times*, is really good at that—she'll add a line about some difficulties she's been having reading this book that she's reviewing. I could have done it, but I didn't.

I don't know whether what she did was a performance or not. I think that a performance involves a gesture, and it can be a gesture of ambivalence, a gesture of confusion … but I couldn't quite see the gesture in what she was doing. I just couldn't, I couldn't see it, it was so confusing, and then the thing at the end that she said seemed to make it clear, that no, in fact, this wasn't a performance, this was a … this was a *problem*. But the other thing was: I didn't want to write about her like a patient. I didn't want to write about her as somebody who was having a crisis, because I don't know about that. I'm not a psychologist, you know? It would be unfair for me and wrong for me to try to get inside somebody's head and diagnose them. I can't do that, I can only try to write about it in as much as it was a performance, and I think that was the thing that really sort of fried my brain. I wasn't sure then, and I'm still not really sure whether it was a performance.

… It wasn't so much about whether or not an individual performance was good or bad, it was like—Chan *represents* something. Chan, and I've never met her, and that's a great record, *Moon Pix*, I really think it's a great record, but to some degree during that period Chan was like a mood. I have a feeling that that's why a lot of people really loved her, because she didn't reduce to songs or albums; she was a mood. These days we think more and more in terms of moods in processing a lot of new culture. But the 1999 version of me had a really hard time with that. I think that within myself, I was like, "look: I'm here for the music. I don't care about this mood. I know you're good, so let's have some good stuff."

10

Cross Bones Style

On Performing

"Sometimes going from one song to the other," Chan says, *"I remember that the audience is there and go into a panic. And I think,* Come on, Chan, what song? What song? *and I can't sing and I can't concentrate and I think,* I hate myself … I'm not a professional entertainer. I'm not Neil Diamond.

Chan interviewed by William Van Meter,
New York Magazine, *2006*

There was always a lot on my mind. You're hoping and praying that you and the audience can meet at the same place, some place that's not here nor there but some "other" place altogether. It's real scary when you're out there by yourself …

Chan interviewed by T. Cole Rachel,
Interview, *2012*

There's a moment, usually around the third song, when there's just this flat line that cuts straight through the room, and our brains are kind of on the same level. It's this energy going both ways. It feels good, you know. The best thing is being able to be accepted and have people say, "Wow, I know exactly how you feel." And that makes me feel less of an outsider, less of an outcast; it makes me stronger. That kid backstage telling me something, and me telling him that I felt the same fucking way and it's completely normal.

Chan interviewed by Roni Sarig,
Creative Loafing, *2003*

Four Views of a Show

Mark

What Did I Just Witness?

The show was at an odd time of day, maybe three or four in the afternoon, sun was pouring in from the windows in the college meeting space. It wasn't a place for shows. Normally the room was divided into three separate rooms, for conferences or something else. This day it was set up like a motivational speaker would be performing: stiff backed chairs in neat rows. There was no opener, no music, just silence. No one announced the show's start, Cat Power just appeared at the front of the room, walked up to the stage through the middle aisle like at a church wedding. There was a sense that no one was facilitating the show; it was just happening.

You knew everyone in the crowd, all music people. It was how you connected with other people. You took a risk buying records; it was a time before people got into the habit of listing things.

A sheet of hair covered her face. Her black jeans and black work shirt countered the brightness of the room.

She played songs one into the next. There weren't always distinct endings, no sense of where to clap. It felt like people were afraid to clap. Sometimes she would pause a song midway through. Other times she would abandon it completely and move on to something else if she felt it was falling apart. There was a palpable sense of: "I'm going to get through this, and then I'm out of here." The room was silent, strangely quiet, stressful, uncomfortable. The crowd looked to each other, hoping that no one would break or heckle or cause harm. We had a silent contract to maintain the awe.

She started packing up her cords and gear. No one was sure that the performance was over. She was acting as it might be, but it was so hard to tell when things were beginning and ending. She walked back down the aisle. Everyone watched her go. She exited out the back of the room, through another door, and went outside. You could see her through the large windows.

She got in a van and drove away. We could all see her drive away. The audience glanced at one another, making eye contact, thinking: "What did I just witness?"

*

Jennifer

The Show Floated around in Our Consciousness

Music is how I met everyone. Word of mouth or a flyer stapled to a kiosk downtown probably told me about the show. Maybe the radio station? There weren't many shows on campus so it was notable. We maybe saw Jesus and Mary Chain or Spiritualized but not much came through campus. It was afternoon in the Ballroom that overlooked the library. Upscale conference seats—roundbacks, cushy—were set up in rows in a single layer, 60/70? No, 50–75 people? The lighting was antiseptic. I think she was late.

You could feel the anticipation.

She came through a door at the front of the room, off to the side where there was a piano. She was dressed a bit heroin chic, T-shirt, black jacket, converse, that's how I remember it. She crumpled around a piano. She was trying to disappear. The sound was really good, so you could hear her self-deprecation clearly, "I don't understand why you're all here when you can see the Dirty Three in St. Louis." She never got comfortable, like she couldn't get past that barrier of discomfort. There were these glittering moments that were amazing. Her voice is just haunting. It was remarkable, different. She played five or six songs, with starts and restarts. It was funny, embarrassing, sad. She didn't give us the chance to hear her.

I could relate to her. I'm a female who loves music. I also have insecurities and am stressed out by it.

In the weeks that followed the show, we talked about it a lot. The show floated around in our consciousness.

*

Tracy

Missed the Show

'96-'98 were the years I lived in Oklahoma City. I was pregnant in '98 and was very particular about what I chose for my baby to hear, and *Moon Pix* was in regular rotation on my boom box. I'd lay in a hammock on our porch with Brittany, Daryle's eleven-year-old daughter, and read the baby name book searching for a middle name for baby Lane, listening to *Moon Pix*, *Ladies and Gentlemen We're Floating in Space* from Spiritualized, and Air's *Moon Safari*. Seems like a million years ago and yesterday.

*

Ben

It Would Almost Be Impossible to See That Kind of Performance Now

Someone convinced me to go.

The room was set up like a boarding school recital. No stage, or lighting, no introduction, sixty or so chairs were lined up in rows. I don't even remember if there was a microphone? She approached the front of the room from the side aisle. She was not discombobulated, not awkward, but it almost seemed painful for her to do what she had to do. It was an excellent performance. She played two or three songs in a row and then would stop; there was no conversation. It seemed like she was contemplating where to go; there was structure but no path. I was impressed by her guitar playing. It was percussive, like she felt the need for a back-up or beat.

She played the Silvertone she always played. It wasn't a full size, it was a ¾ size, a catalog guitar that you could buy in the '60s and '70s from Montgomery Ward and Sears.

The audience was dead quiet, attentive. There were no interruptions or disruptions.

To me it's the struggle that's so awesome … that fragility and struggle. We all have that and it's nice to see. It was the kind of performance that leaves the fan with a connection that you feel *at that time*, sort of mirroring how that person feels the things, and you can relate. It's what you want when you see a performer as far as being exposed, open, emotional. Newer music is so formulaic; it would almost be impossible to see that kind of performance now.

11

Peking Saint

Revisiting the Album Twenty Years Later

Looking back, it seems like Cat Power's Moon Pix *only registered as a minor breakthrough on its release in 1998. Few immediately hailed it as a masterpiece, and few anticipated it would become the influential work it's since grown into. Perhaps because it remained unhobbled by praise and expectation,* Moon Pix *grew in stature in the ensuing twenty years …*
Scott Wallace, Sydney Scoop, *2018*

… Maybe Moon Pix *was an influential album; I don't really know. I could certainly imagine plenty of other young women hearing this young woman singing of darkness and demons and hell with such vulnerability and such power, and I can imagine them being inspired to try making music themselves. But I never heard another album like* Moon Pix, *from Cat Power or anyone else. And in the two decades*

that have followed, indie rock has largely moved away from trying to capture that sense of the uncanny, of worlds beyond the one we can see.

Tom Briehan, Stereogum, *2018*

… But what Marshall does on Moon Pix *was equally important: She pours her heart and soul out for public consumption. By doing so, she sets an example of how to talk about weakness without feeling ashamed—which went entirely against the idea being packaged and sold to women and girls in 1998.* Moon Pix *is a gift of a record from start to finish, and it will continue to work its magic, healing metal hearts, for generations to come.*

Lisa Lagace, NPR, *2017*

With Moon Pix, *Marshall made a name for herself alongside the likes of Elliott Smith and Neutral Milk Hotel's Jeff Mangum, with dark music that isn't traditionally pretty, and doesn't romanticize her own sadness. She became known for her blood-and-guts lyrics in a way that few other women had in that particular era of indie-folk …*

… Cat Power—and Moon Pix *in particular—exemplifies what it means to be a woman and to feel fucked up … but not in a beautiful, glamorous way.*

Annie Fell, Riot Fest, *2018*

Pitchfork *updated its score from 7.4 to 9.5.*

The Author on Moon Pix

The Album Cover

In 1998, I was in high school in New Jersey. It was a beachfront city which, at its height, was a flaunted shore town where Winslow Homer painted and seven American presidents vacationed. At its lowest, some sort of riot happened in 1994 caused by a combination of things. Depending on who you spoke to the "riot" was due to: rumors of a police shooting, racism, a shady mayoral race, a child's death, or a crackdown on drug dealers including implementation of the "Jump Out Boys" (a renegade group of cops meant to, literally, jump out at crime). The town was on a spectrum of wealth, one friend raised rabbits in their hallway for dinner, another was getting solar panels installed before that was a thing. My family was somewhere in the middle of all of this. We lived in a duplex and shared a whole wall with other people.

Indie rock didn't really take at my high school as there wasn't really a critical mass of any one culture or subculture. I asked two people from high school about this recently on Facebook, wondering if this was just my imagination, one said, "It was like every other place, what do you mean?" Another said something like, "We were different but it didn't matter. I don't know, we just were." The closest I got to indie rock was a few goth-y girls who would carve their boyfriend's names into their skin and learned about Sonic Youth during their stay at a mental hospital. I listened to the radio, FM 106.3 (the original home of *120 Minutes* host Matt Pinfield), and would also listen to 88.9, a local college radio station with one indie rock DJ (I think his name was Skiz? Maybe with two "z"s? Skizz?).

I befriended a group of kids a few towns over, kids who lived in a wealthy neighborhood where the thrift shops had better stuff and where kids could afford to listen to anything they wanted. We would hang out in Red Bank, NJ, where Director Kevin Smith had a comic book shop. There were a few vintage stores, more than one coffee shop, and Jack's Music where sometimes you could see Bruce Springsteen flipping through the extensive rows of CDs. Red Bank also had one of the first internet cafes around; my friend would drag me to open mics to see her crush, who would cover Incubus songs on acoustic guitar. Gross. We would also go to Black Cat Records, a small record store whose workers wore things like black baby-doll tees or little page boy hats and heavily tattooed arms. At this point, vinyl was cheaper than CDs, not by much but enough to get my parent's turntable working. *Moon Pix* looked at me from a shelf. Chan Marshall's face peeked out from behind some kind of flowering tree. What was she looking at? What could she tell me? I wanted to know.

The Show

My boyfriend at the time (featured in Chapter 5) had a stepfather who was a talent agent or something (no one knows what their parents or stepparents do all day). What we did know was that he owned a fraction of a racehorse and that he could get us tickets to nearly any show we wanted, a perk we discovered far too late in our high school years. Some strange trust on behalf of my mother (mixed with my father's early-onset dementia) allowed me to go to shows at a young age. The legendary Stone Pony in Asbury Park was close by; I saw Juliana Hatfield, Wesley Willis, Weezer, and so many more. Matador was having a tenth-anniversary concert in New York, the Matador Tour, three days of label lineups. Pavement's time was running out. *Terror Twilight* had just released, and—I can't remember whether it was rumor or fact—we were pretty sure it was our last chance to see them. The lineup included Guitar Wolf, Chavez, Cat Power (solo), and Pavement. My boyfriend drove us into the city.

The show was at Irving Plaza, a dull club that I remember nothing about. Guitar Wolf opened, a weird choice given their intense, alienating, alien punk rock, which confused the small, early crowd. Why wasn't Chavez more famous? As a short person, I could barely see anything, let alone Cat Power. Things were even cloudier in pre-smoking ban New York. Chan covered "Satisfaction" by The Rolling Stones (which I only recognized because my boyfriend pointed it out) in a slow, methodical rhythm and a voice that made you listen to what the song was about: the aching, lonely, unfulfilling nature of life under capitalism which, as a teen, resonated. I distinctly remember a group of college-aged boys wearing backwards baseball hats screaming, "Rock out!" at Chan repeatedly. (Years later, I would see Bill Callahan, and a version of these boys was there, now wearing ties with unbuttoned collars, screaming, "This song is about sex!") Chan tuned her guitar a lot and wouldn't look at any of us. *Moon Pix* took on a different tone for me now, hearing it as an opposition to "Rock out," a stance against the forced *anything* that someone wants someone else to do or be.

The Video, Internet & Reading

At the show, my boyfriend bought the *What's Up Matador?* VHS music video compilation, a thing that taught me about image, sex, and power even more than it taught me about music. My boyfriend drooled at a lipstick-smeared Mary Timony. I mimicked Cat Power's line dance moves from "Cross Bones Style." We both tried to decipher Solex. "Cross Bones" looked like a Gap ad circulating on TV around then, with the white backdrop and dancing. Still, it felt like something else, another way to look and be, a different kind of religion being offered through its methodical movement. As the interviewee in Chapter 4 pointed out to me during our conversation, this time for me as a teenage girl must have been pivotal.

My dad was always hyper-aware of tech. He had an Atari early on and would get me (himself) Nintendos. Eventually, we got a computer. My first AOL handle was pencapchew3, a vague Nirvana reference. I didn't hang out online much, a few pop-ins to chat rooms about indie film or music, attempts to track down *Eraserhead* on VHS on early eBay, but I never felt a connection to the internet, a need for it. It was a feeling I had offline as well. Living in a place where there was an abnormal shared experience, and genuine attempts at understanding, didn't make me ache to be a part of some specific online place because I felt, in some way, a part of everything. However, magazines did act as a connection to places outside of my hometown. The weekly or monthly pages arrived in our mailbox outlining what was happening over there in New York, pages that truly shaped my ideas of art, image, and culture. I fervently read *Paper* magazine and *Time Out New York* (totally unaware that the interviewee in Chapter 6 was responsible for my whole perception of music writing). I cut out the pictures and made collages with lots of lips and eyeballs, enduring teen girl semiotics. Chan Marshall would occasionally pop up in a magazine; I was glad she was still wearing T-shirts but didn't begrudge her interest in fashion which was growing alongside my own.

Writing

The Covers Record was fine, but (like Matador) I wanted a new *Moon Pix*, something to guide me through this new, weird stage of post-adolescence. I got a copy of *You Are Free*. There was something slightly blunt and distant in the album. It felt fitting for the post 9/11 coldness that was acute in Northern New Jersey at the time. Someone in a college class of mine, a skinny kid we listened to because he spent a Summer in France, told me to write for the *Rutgers Review*, an on-campus arts and entertainment paper. The office was on the upper floors of the student center, a fossilized computer with an early version of Quark sat to the side, a gross striped couch was squishy with more than foam. The first thing I ever wrote was a review of *You Are Free*; I wrote under a male pen name to hide from judgment. I only remember one thing about that review, mainly because someone quoted it back to me, not knowing I was the author. I compared Chan's voice to a fluorescent light that could turn you on or off, a sharp balance of bright and dim that beckoned you closer while pushing you away. That creative push and pull from *Moon Pix* was still a part of Cat Power, a desire to be seen yet also obscured.

New York

At the end of college, I moved to Greenpoint, Brooklyn. I had money saved from a summer job and had two months to find a new job before I had no money. I knew nothing about the neighborhood at all, just that it was cheap at the time, and when I got off the G train, everyone looked like my Polish grandparents. I was living in a box factory with illegal lofts surrounding it, followed by a prefab apartment building in Bushwick made to meet the demand for housing in the gentrifying area.

I didn't know it but I stepped into the fading memories and ghosts of the LES scene. Many LES residents had escaped to Greenpoint after being priced out by gentrification. I was in an art show at Max Fish (the Orchard St. location, not the original Ludlow one), but I had no idea what Max Fish was, and when I went there, I didn't know anyone and left. I followed my roommate into TG-170 where a tiny dog greeted me, and the clothes were all too expensive, telling me I didn't belong. I went to clubs, many of which had changed addresses to newer, affordable locations.

Many years later, I saw Cat Power again, this time at the Hiro Ballroom in Manhattan. Someone I knew from work invited me at the last minute. Hiro was a bar venue in Chelsea inside a hotel that looked like a ship on the outside. I always wondered what was in there. The sleek room had shiny wood, red lanterns, a faint Japanese styling. Cat Power came out and sat behind a piano. She told everyone she was happy. She was in a good mood. She asked us all to sit on the floor, and the entire room humbly complied. It felt like we were sitting in her living room. Some drunk dude kept professing his love to her, "Will you marry me?" to which she replied that her bodyguard was backstage, Irish, and hadn't had a drink in seventeen years and that she'd be happy to bring him out. Her banter was playful and acknowledged the unnatural reality of the situation with ease. The show was joyous, precise, lush; the mournful quality of Chan's voice could be heard, but it didn't make you want to cry. It made you want to smile. She covered Gnarls Barkley's "Crazy" with sincerity and swagger.

This Book

I had reached out to Chan's manager a few times when writing this book, accomplishing nothing other than putting the book on their radar and them asking to fact check it. How do you fact-check a book that is based on a music legend? How do you verify words when they no longer stand still? Or when they exist purely for marketing? There is a person, Chan Marshall, at the center of the album, sure, an artist who was interviewed exhaustively in the press and has a recollection of their own experiences but it's the collective memories that form Cat Power. It's the people living the culture that make it.

When I pitched this book, it was right before the beginning of the Covid-19 pandemic, about a month before lockdowns which altered everything about what I was writing. I would begin each interview with, "Is everything okay?" I had no prepared statement for the response and found myself holding my breath as I waited for the answer. I suddenly became connected to these strangers through a different story, one beyond *Moon Pix*. Many people asked why I was writing this book, especially as someone not steeped in fan culture. *Moon Pix* has always been on the periphery of my vision, in short, intense bursts of memories that deeply affected who I think I am. Some of those bursts are told here as stories, others are mine to keep. Other stories in this book don't belong to me; I've distilled them down to a new story, maybe to question or better understand a larger one? Some stories are documents, some are documentaries. Other stories are advertisements, diaries, or even data. Many stories are myths. It's a constant collective act to choose what stories are listened to, how they will be told and what stories are to be believed.

*

Moon Pix was my salvation as a very mixed-up young person. And suddenly I see that.

Chan Marshall, The Guardian, 2018

Annotated Bibliography

Chapter 1: American Flag

The main sources used in this chapter were articles on the Echo Project in South Carolina and interviews with Chan Marshall in which she talked about the making of the album, her time in Australia and touring. Dozens of tiny mentions here and there were pieced together to try to make a larger picture of what the experience might have been like. Note: Due to computer overheating, sites were re-accessed when writing the bibliography.

Bragg, Ricky. "In South Carolina, a Klan Museum Opens Old Wounds." *The New York Times*. Originally Published November 17,1996. Accessed January 20, 2022. 199https://www.nytimes.com/1996/11/17/us/in-a-south-carolina-town-a-klan-museum-opens-old-wounds.html

Carew, Anthony. *Interview with Chan. Gravity Girls* via Ode to Chan 1998. Accessed July 14, 2021. https://odetochan.forumgratuit.org/t5-moon-pix-1998

Collins, Jeffrey. "Pastor's Fight against KKK Becomes Movie That May Aid Battle." *Associated Press*. January 29, 2020. https://apnews.com/article/us-news-ap-top-news-sc-state-wire-south-carolina-movies-6070e0d47a9b510d173ce33b867dee9c

Collins, Jeffrey. "Work Begins to Turn SC Racist Store into Racial Harmony Site." *ABC News*. December 31, 2020. https://abcnews.go.com/US/wireStory/work-begins-turn-sc-racist-store-racial-harmony-74986817

Daprile, Lucas. "It Once Housed KKK Robes, Swastikas. Now a Laurens Pastor Is Planning a Diversity Center." *Greenville News*. November 26, 2018. https://www.greenvilleonline.com/story/news/2018/11/26/laurens-countys-shuttered-redneck-shop-eyed-diversity-center/2114352002/

Dornan, Matt. "Cat Power." *Comes with a Smile* #5, Summer 2000. Accessed July 14, 2021. https://cwas.hinah.com/interview/?id=15

Goodman, Elizabeth. *Cat Power: A Good Woman*. Crown, 2009. Google Play.

Hennessy, Kate. "Cat Power on Moon Pix: I'm Alive Today because of those Songs." *The Guardian*. May 27, 2018. https://www.theguardian.com/music/2018/may/28/cat-power-on-moon-pix-im-alive-today-because-of-those-songs

Kelley, Trevor. "From the Archives: Cat Power, November, 2005." *Trevorkelley's Blog*. January 2, 2009. https://trevorkelley.wordpress.com/2009/01/02/hello-world/

Kellner, Amy. "Chan Marshall." *Index*. 1998. Accessed July 5, 2021. http://www.indexmagazine.com/interviews/chan_marshall.shtml

Maida, Marcus. "Catpower—Maybe Not Music, Maybe Something Else." *Hotel Discipline*. http://hoteldiscipline.net/?page_id=366

Page, Sydney. "Once He 'World's Only Klan Museum', It Is Becoming a Center for History and Healing." *The Washington Post*. January 8, 2021. https://www.washingtonpost.com/lifestyle/2021/01/08/kkk-museum-redneck-race-healing/

Weeks, Greg. "Article by Greg Weeks." *Sand from the Urns*. 1998. Posted on Alain Serrano's Cat Power Page. Accessed July 5, 2021. http://alain.serrano.pagesperso-orange.fr/perso/catpower/InterviewGregWeeks.html

Chapter 2: He Turns Down

In a documentary film I always found it startling how questions are removed; the viewer is left with the answers as if unprompted. I wanted that feeling, that weird false spontaneity. I also found quotes from interviews with Chan about her experience making the album, sometimes they collide or clash.

Matt Voigt in conversation with the author, March 2021.

Ballam-Cross, Paul. "Sing Sing South, Sing Sing East: The Continuing Legacy of Australia's Famed Recording Studio." *Reverb*. August 29, 2018. https://reverb.com/news/sing-sing-south-sing-sing-east-the-continuing-legacy-of-australias-famed-recording-studio

Carew, Anthony. Interview with Chan. *Gravity Girls*, Ode to Chan 1998. Accessed July 14, 2021. https://odetochan.forumgratuit.org/t5-moon-pix-1998

Dornan, Matt. "Cat Power." Comes With a Smile #4. Winter 1998/9. The Lost Issue. Accessed December 10, 2021. https://cwas.hinah.com/interview/?id=13

Kellner, Amy. "Chan Marshall." *Index*. 1998. Accessed July 5, 2021. http://www.indexmagazine.com/interviews/chan_marshall.shtml

O'Hara, Gail. Chan Marshall. chickfactor #10. 1999. Accessed January 20, 2022. https://www.chickfactor.com/interviews/chan-marshall/

"Sing Sing Studios." *Mixdown*. Accessed January 22, 2022. https://mixdownmag.com.au/features/backstage/dax-liniere-of-puzzle-factory/

"Sing Sing Studios." *Youtube*, uploaded by Audio Technology Magazine. March 22, 2010. https://www.youtube.com/watch?v=qk4yziiFa4k

Teague, Marcus. "How a Part-Time Melbourne Engineer Recorded a Cat Power Classic." *Broadsheet*. May 29, 2018. https://www.broadsheet.com.au/sydney/entertainment/article/how-part-time-melbourne-engineer-recorded-cat-power-classic
Weeks, Greg. "Article by Greg Weeks." *Sand from the Urns*. 1998. Accessed July 5, 2021. http://alain.serrano.pagesperso-orange.fr/perso/catpower/InterviewGregWeeks.html

Chapter 3: No Sense

It's hard to explain a feeling and New York City is very much a feeling. It's also hard to explain gentrification—those moments when something is wild and free and then slowly becomes an expensive mirror. I interviewed a few people about NYC; how it felt in the '90s, what it was like, how it was changing, and read a lot about it as well.

New York/Chan.
Edward Douglas in discussion with the author, February 2021.
Michael Galinsky in discussion with the author, March 2021 and July 2021.

Blush, Steven. *"New York Rock: From the Rise of the Velvet Underground to the Fall of CBGB."* Griffin an imprint of St. Martin's Press. 2016.
Brooks of Sheffield. "This Was Ludlow Street." *Lost City*. Blogger. April 10, 2008. http://lostnewyorkcity.blogspot.com/2008/04/this-was-ludlow-street.html
Carlson, Jen. "Here's How Different the Lower East Side Looked in 1995." *Gothamist*. January 23, 2015. https://gothamist.com/arts-entertainment/heres-how-different-the-lower-east-side-looked-in-1995

Cat Power. Wikipedia, Wikimedia Foundation Inc. January 10, 2022. https://en.wikipedia.org/wiki/Cat_Power

Dallas, Paul. "Politics of Style: Restoring and Rediscovering Apparatus Films." *Filmmaker Magazine*. October 20, 2016. https://filmmakermagazine.com/100247-politics-of-style/#.Yem67mBMHrB

Detrick, Ben. "Watching 'The Fish' Fade to Black." *The New York Times*. December 15, 2010. https://www.nytimes.com/2010/12/16/fashion/16maxfish.html

Friedlander, Emilie. "A Walking Tour of Manhattan's Rock 'n'Roll Past: the 2000s." *The New York Times*. November 20, 2018. https://www.nytimes.com/2018/11/20/arts/music/indie-rock-walking-tour-manhattan.html

Gates, Kenny. "Matador Records Founder Chris Lombardi In Founding an Indie Label, 'Signing Music You Love.'" *Hypebot*. January 27, 2017. https://www.hypebot.com/hypebot/2017/01/we-sign-music-we-love-the-matador-origin-story-interview.html

Hill, Logan, et al. "My New York Places That Changed Us." *New York Magazine*. December 18, 2000. https://nymag.com/nymetro/realestate/neighborhoods/features/4180/

Jen, Rev. *Elf Girl*. Simon & Schuster/Gallery Books, 2011.

Kelly, Matt. "Cat power." Cool Beans #7. Accessed December 10, 2021. http://coolbeans.com/cb7/catpower.htm

Larocca, Amy. *Folk Heroine*. New York Magazine. August 27, 2001. https://nymag.com/shopping/articles/fallfashion2001/catpower.htm

Lower East Side. Wikipedia, Wikimedia Foundation Inc. June 25, 2021. https://en.wikipedia.org/wiki/Lower_East_Side

McCormick, Carlo. "Exile on Ludlow St." *Zing Magazine*. 2001. Accessed July 14, 2021. https://www.aaronrose.co/alleged-gallery

Murphy, Tom. "Cat Power's Chan Marshall on Sun: ' I didn't want to test myself so much as push myself." *Westworld*.

November 13, 2013. https://www.westword.com/music/cat-powers-chan-marshall-on-sun-i-didnt-want-to-test-myself-so-much-as-push-myself-5677364

Pham, Diane. "The Urban Lens: Ash Thayer's Poignant Photographs of '90s Lower East Side Squatters." *6sqft*. September 8, 2017. https://www.6sqft.com/the-urban-lens-ash-thayers-poignant-photographs-of-90s-lower-east-side-squatters/

Rickman, James, and Thompson, Elizabeth. "An Oral History of Max Fish." *Paper*. October, 2013.

Sanneh, Kelefa. "Fish Tales." *The New Yorker*. February 27, 2011. https://www.newyorker.com/magazine/2011/03/07/fish-tales

Shaff, Corey. "2B: Art Space in East Village 1995." *Vimeo*. October 14, 2011. https://vimeo.com/30571810

Shaff, Corey. "Planet Ludlow: Ludlow Street 1995." *Vimeo*. October 14, 2011. https://vimeo.com/30576998

Weaver, Shaye. "'Walk on the Wild Side' Tours Retrace the Humble Beginnings of Sonic Youth, Madonna, Basquiat and More." *amNY*. August 29, 2018. https://www.amny.com/entertainment/things-to-do/walk-on-the-wild-side-nyc-tour-1-20723602/

Zahm, Olivier. "Chan Marshall: The Only One." *Purple Magazine*, F/W 2012, Iss. 18. Accessed July 14, 2021. https://purple.fr/magazine/fw-2012-issue-18/chan-marshall/

New York/Michael Galinsky

Michael Galinsky in discussion with the author July 2021.

Cosloy, Gerard. Wikipedia, Wikimedia Foundation Inc. January 6, 2022. https://en.wikipedia.org/wiki/Gerard_Cosloy

The Editors of *Encyclopedia Britannica*. "Roger Corman: American Writer and Director." *Encyclopedia Britannica online*. Accessed July 15, 2021. https://www.britannica.com/biography/Roger-Corman

Frances, Susan. "Filmmakers Michael Galinsky & Suki Hawley Half-Cocked Again." *Glide Magazine*. January 18, 2007.

https://glidemagazine.com/9032/filmmakers-michael-galinsky-and-suki-hawley/

Galinsky, Michael. "When Photography Develops into Documentary." Documentary Magazine. December 31, 2004. https://www.documentary.org/feature/when-photography-develops-documentary

Half-Cocked. Directed Suki Hawley. Rumur, 1994. 90min.

Hanley, Steven T. "The Lonesome Crowded West: An Interview with Michael Galinsky." *Fanzine*. December 14, 2015. http://thefanzine.com/the-lonesome-crowded-west-an-interview-with-michael-galinsky/

Hawley, Suki. Wikipedia, Wikimedia Foundation Inc. April 25, 2021. https://en.wikipedia.org/wiki/Suki_Hawley

Radiation. Directed by Michael Galinsky and Suki Hawley. Radiation Pictures. 1999. 85min.

Smithson, Aline. "Michael Galinsky: The Decline of Mall Civilization." *Lenscratch*. November 30, 2019. http://lenscratch.com/2019/11/michael-galinsky-the-decline-of-mall-civilization/

Weisbard, Eric. "The Graying of Indie Rock." *The Village Voice*. March 23, 1999. https://www.villagevoice.com/1999/03/23/the-graying-of-indie-rock/

Internet

Baym, Nancy K. *Playing to the Crowd: Musicians, Audiences and the Intimate Work of Connection*. NYU Press, 2018.

Lepore, Jill. "The Cobweb." *The New Yorker*. January 19, 2015. https://www.newyorker.com/magazine/2015/01/26/cobweb

Matadorrec.com. Internet Archive: Wayback Machine. *Alexa Crawls*. Archived February 10, 1999. https://web.archive.org/web/19990210074829/http://matadorrec.com/bands/bands.html

Milks, Megan. *Tori Amos Bootleg Webring: Remember the Internet no. 2*. Instar Books. 2021.

One Terabyte of Kilobyte Age: Digging through the Geocities Torrent. https://blog.geocities.institute/

Skipworth, Hunter. "World Photography Day 2014: The history of digital cameras." *DigitalSpy*. August 19, 2014. https://www.digitalspy.com/tech/cameras/a591251/world-photography-day-2014-the-history-of-digital-cameras/

New York/Roe

Berner, Sooanne. "Where Glossy Fashion Photography and Family Albums Collide." *AnOther*. November 3, 2016. https://www.anothermag.com/fashion-beauty/9236/uniting-art-life-and-commerce-roe-ethridge-s-new-photobook

Bush, Kate. *All Systems Go: The Art of Roe Ethridge*. Artforum. October, 2003. https://www.artforum.com/print/200308/all-systems-go-the-art-of-roe-ethridge-5488

Crum-Tesfa, Zoma. *Roe Ethridge's Forgotten Neighbors*. SSense. Accessed January 10, 2022. https://www.ssense.com/en-us/editorial/culture/roe-ethridges-forgotten-neighbors

"ICA Speaks: Roe Ethridge (Full Lecture)." *Institute of Contemporary Art Miami, ICA Speaks*. https://icamiami.org/video/ica-speaks-roe-ethridge-full-lecture/

"In Conversation Roe Ethridge and Antwaun Sargent." *Gagosian Quarterly*. April 27, 2020. https://gagosian.com/quarterly/2020/04/27/interview-roe-ethridge-and-antwaun-sargent/

Herndon, Lara Kristin. "Body in Peril: The Photographs of Roe Ethridge." *Cover Our Tracks*. February 22, 2018. https://www.coverourtracks.com/single-post/2018/02/22/body-in-peril-the-photographs-of-roe-ethridge

Lange, Christy. "For This Thing to Happen." *Frieze*, Issue 150. October 1, 2012. https://www.frieze.com/article/thing-happen

Lim, James. *Depth of Field: Photographer Roe Ethridge on Shooting for Dazed & Confused, Kenzo and Goldman Sachs*. The Cut.

March 6, 2012. https://www.thecut.com/2012/03/studio-visit-roe-ethridge.html

"Roe Ethridge in Conversation with Kevin Moore." Uploaded by School of Visual Arts. *YouTube*. April 20, 2016. https://www.youtube.com/watch?v=JeOqQoxwjhc

Vice Staff. *An Interview with Roe Ethridge*. Vice. July 15, 2010. https://www.vice.com/en/article/yvnaqw/an-interview-with-roe-ethridge

Chapter 4: Say

All interviews were edited by the author and then sent to the interviewees for edits. I want people to sound human but I also want them to be comfortable in their representation. This section also includes comments inspired by actual comments on the music video for "Cross Bones Style" on the internet. Some sources from Chapter 1 were also consulted for this section.

Brett Vapnek in conversation with the author, May 2021.

Breihan, Tom. "Moon Pix Turns 20." *Stereogum*. September 21, 2018. https://www.stereogum.com/2015198/cat-power-moon-pix/reviews/the-anniversary/

"Cat Power—'Cross Bones Style.'" Uploaded by Matador Records. *YouTube*. October 23, 2017. https://www.youtube.com/watch?v=aW2PcOyAWwM

Cross Bones Style Cat Power. Song Meanings. Accessed July 11, 2021. https://songmeanings.com/songs/view/59099/

Macaulay, Scott. "25 New Faces of Independent Film." *Filmmaker Magazine*. Accessed July 11, 2021. https://filmmakermagazine.com/archives/issues/summer2001/features/25_faces6-10.php

Silvercup Studios. Accessed July 11, 2021. https://www.
    silvercupstudios.com/history
Brett Vapnek. *Vimeo Userpage*. Vimeo. https://vimeo.com/user298725

Chapter 5: Metal Heart

When I started this book, I did not know that *Moon Pix* was an album
written around the time of Chan's relationship with Bill Callahan and
that his album, *Knock, Knock*, was the same. These two albums were
on repeat throughout my life. How did I not know this? How does
something get branded a breakup album? How do people find out?
Who decides that it is? Thank you ex-boyfriends willing to participate.

Brian in conversation with the author via Facebook Messenger,
    March 2021.
Charles in conversation with the author via Zoom. March 2021.
Ted in conversation with the author via Zoom. March 2021.
Goodman, Elizabeth. *Cat Power: A Good Woman*. Crown, 2009.
    Google Play.
Kelley, Trevor. "From the Archives: Cat Power, November, 2005."
    Trevorkelley's Blog. January 2, 2009. https://trevorkelley.
    wordpress.com/2009/01/02/hello-world/
Maida, Marcus Maida. "Catpower—Maybe Not Music, Maybe
    Something Else." *Hotel Discipline*. http://hoteldiscipline.
    net/?page_id=366
Scott, Tim. "Bill Callahan Goes Deep on His Classic Track 'River
    Guard.'" *Vice*. April 30, 2017. https://www.vice.com/en/article/
    vvapam/bill-callahan-goes-deep-on-his-classic-track-river-guard
Sherburne, Philip. "Smog: Knock, Knock." *Pitchfork*. August 2, 2020.
    https://pitchfork.com/reviews/albums/smog-knock-knock/

Weeks, Greg. NYC. 1998. "Sand from the Urns." Accessed July 5, 2021. http://alain.serrano.pagesperso-orange.fr/perso/catpower/InterviewGregWeeks.html

Chapter 6: Back of Your Head

Music reviews are always a type of writing I love: How do you explain in written word something that is heard? How can one distill a life's work down into a star or number or letter grade? Note: Some of these web archives have conflicting captures.

Gail O'Hara in conversation with the author, June 2021.

Alex T. Moore E-mail conversation with author, June 2021.

Bailey, Stuart. "Cat Power—Moon Pix." *NME*, Internet Archive: WayBack Machine. September 16, 1998. Archived from the original on August 17, 2000. Retrieved May 11, 2016. https://web.archive.org/web/20000817214118/http://www.nme.com/reviews/reviews/19980816142159reviews.html

Christgau, Robert. "Consumer Guide: Turkey Shoot." Posted on Robert Christgau: Dean of American Rock Critics via *The Village Voice* December 1, 1998. http://www.robertchristgau.com/xg/cg/ts98-98.php

Dark, Jane. "Gray Line-Off Rhythm." *The Village Voice*, vol. 43, no. 39, p. 67. September 29, 1998. https://www.villagevoice.com/1998/09/29/gray-line-off-rhyme/

Fricke, David, and Rob, Sheffield. "The Year in Recordings." *Rolling Stone*, no. 802/803, December 1998, p. 160. EBSCOhost,search.ebscohost.com/login.aspx?direct=true&db=f5h&AN=1410578&site=eds-live&scope=site

Moore, Alex T. "Cat Power: Moon Pix (Matador)." *The Rutgers Review*, December 8, 1998.

O'Hara, Gail. "Cat Power: Bowery Ballroom; Friday October 30." *Time Out New York*, October 29–November 4, 1998.

Schreiber, Ryan. "Cat Power *Moon Pix*." *Pitchforkmedia*, WayBackMachine. Archived August 16, 2000. http://web. archive.org/web/20000816164713/www.pitchforkmedia.com/ record-reviews/c/cat-power/moon-pix.shtml

Trew, Jonathan. "Cat Power Moon Pix (Matador)." *The List*, Issue 343. September 24, 1998. https://archive.list.co.uk/the-list/1998-09-24/47/

van Dorston, A.S. "Cat Power-Moon Pix (Matador, 1998)." *Fast "n" Bulbous*. September 22, 1998. https://fastnbulbous.com/cat-power-moon-pix/

Vaziri, Aidin. "Cat Power's 'Moon' Light as a Whisper." *Chron*. October 11, 1998. Updated February 3, 2012. https://www.chron. com/music/article/An-Emotional-Ode-to-Garland-2986110.php

Chapter 7: Moonshiner

If the Wikipedia entry says something is disputed, it is most definitely so. By no means is this an exhaustive chronology of the folk/traditional "Moonshiner" but it's a version of one that I can imagine. I kept getting angry at this chapter as some of the research aspects were financially prohibitive—the only bio of Delia Murphy was retailing online for over $200. The price of facts is a scary thing; they have always been costly (newspapers cost money, magazines too), but as the value of truth rises how can facts remain accessible? I've turned to libraries throughout my life but even then it is hard to access certain info, especially the non-digitized (the pandemic of 2020 also threw a wrench into physical media access). The internet is a fleeting beast of information. Who knows when a website will disappear or when it will be archived? Collective understanding feels far out of reach.

Autopsy IV. "From Irish Folk Tine to Alt. Country Stalwart: A Moonshiner's Journey." *Nine Bullets*. Wordpress. April 8, 2008. http://ninebullets.net/archives/from-irish-folk-tune-to-altcountry-stalwart-a-moonshiners-journey

GUEST, Hugh Walter Jennings. "Origins: Origin of Moonshiner." *The Mudcat Cafe*. October 13. Accessed July 14, 2021. https://mudcat.org/thread.cfm?threadid=95516

The Moonshiner. Wikipedia, Wikimedia Foundation Inc. Last updated March 23, 2021. https://en.wikipedia.org/wiki/The_Moonshiner

Tsk. "Moonshiner." *Second Hand Songs*. Accessed July 14, 2021. https://secondhandsongs.com/work/113412/versions

Chan Marshall

Horton, Kaleb. "The Music That Made Cat Power's Chan Marshall." *Pitchfork*. October 3, 2018. https://pitchfork.com/features/5-10-15-20/the-music-that-made-cat-powers-chan-marshall/

Marcus, Greil. "What Goes on Under the Covers." *Interview Magazine*. January 1999.

Rachel, T. Cole. "Cat Power." *Interview Magazine*. July 22, 2012. https://www.interviewmagazine.com/music/cat-power

Bob Dylan

Gray, Michael. Alan Lomax 95 Today. *Bob Dylan Encyclopedia: A Blog 2006–2012*. January 31, 2010. http://www.michaelgray.net/dylan-blog.html

Petrus, Stephen. Bob Dylan's New York. 1961. *The Gotham Center for New York Art History*. April 19, 2017. https://www.gothamcenter.org/blog/bob-dylans-new-york-1961

Rotolo, Suze. *A Freewheelin' Time: A Memoir of Greenwich Village in the 60s*. Broadway Books an imprint of The Doubleday Publishing Group. New York. 2008.

The Waltons

All About the Waltons, Facebook. January 5, 2017. https://www.
facebook.com/AllAboutTheWaltons/videos/moonshiner-jason-
walton/1776771485918525/

Season Seven Ep. 9 The Beau. *All about the Waltons*. Accessed
December 10, 2021. http://www.allaboutthewaltons.com/ep-s7/
s07-09.php

The Waltons. Wikipedia, Wikimedia Foundation Inc. July 13, 2021.
https://en.wikipedia.org/wiki/The_Waltons#Production

Dave Van Ronk

Browne, David. "Meet the Folk Singer Who Inspired 'Inside Llewyn
Davis.'" *Rolling Stone*. December 2, 2013. https://www.rollingstone.
com/music/music-news/meet-the-folk-singer-who-inspired-inside-
llewyn-davis-243730/

Inside Llewyn Davis. Directed by Ethan & Joel Coen. Studiocanal, 2013.

Johnkatsmc5. "Barbara Muller 'Double Premiere' Private US
1964 Psych Folk." Johnkatsmc5, Blogger. July 23, 2016.
https://johnkatsmc5.blogspot.com/2016/07/barbara-muller-
double-premiere-private.html

Rotolo, Suze. *A Freewheelin' Time: A Memoir of Greenwich Village
in the 60s*. Broadway Books an imprint of The Doubleday
Publishing Group. New York. 2008.

van Ronk, Dave. Wikipedia, Wikimedia Foundation Inc. July 3,
2021. https://en.wikipedia.org/wiki/Dave_Van_Ronk

Barbara Müller and Wendy Caesar

Müller, Barbara and Caesar, Wendy. "Friday Evening Performances
at the 1978 Florida Folk Festival (Main Stage) (Reel 2)." *Florida
Memory State Library and Archives of Florida*. Accessed July 13,
2021. https://www.floridamemory.com/items/show/239043

Johnkatsmc5." Barbara Muller 'Double Premiere' Private US 1964."
Johnkatsmc5, the experience of music. Blogger. July 23, 2016.

https://johnkatsmc5.blogspot.com/2016/07/barbara-muller-double-premiere-private.html

Karen Dalton

Karen Dalton: In My Own Time. Directed by Richard Peete & Robert Yapkowitz. Light in the Attic Records, 2020.

Wertheimer, Linda. "Karen Dalton: A Reluctant Voice Rediscovered." *NPR*. July 12, 2008. https://www.npr.org/templates/story/story.php?storyId=92456345

Rolf Cahn

Cahn, Rolf. Wikipedia, Wikimedia Foundation Inc. April 2, 2021. https://en.wikipedia.org/wiki/Rolf_Cahn

Hannan, Ross and Arnold, Corry. *Berkeley*. September 13, 2011. http://www.chickenonaunicycle.com/Berkeley%20Art.htm

The Clancys and Tommy Makem

Clancy, Liam. *The Mountain of the Women: Memoirs of an Irish Troubadour*. Doubleday a division of Random House. New York. 2002.

The Clancy Brothers. Wikipedia, Wikimedia Foundation Inc. January 27, 2021. https://en.wikipedia.org/wiki/The_Clancy_Brothers

Delia Murphy

Browne, Ronan. "Delia Murphy." Accessed December 10, 2021. http://www.ronanbrowne.com/deliamurphy/Delia_Murphy/Delia_Murphy.html

Darrenst. "Delia Murphy-The Moonshiner/The Roving Journeyman." *Discogs*. Accessed July 13, 2021. https://www.discogs.com/Delia-Murphy-The-Moonshiner-The-Roving-Journeyman/release/13206133 Mayo Ireland, 2019. https://www.mayo-ireland.ie/en/about-mayo/people/delia-murphy.html

"Delia Murphy, 'Ballad Queen,' People from Co. Mayo." *Mayo Ireland*. Accessed December 10, 2021. https://www.mayo-ireland.ie/en/about-mayo/people/delia-murphy.html

Mickey & Mary Carton

Alex. Mickey and Mary Carton and Their Orchestra.
The Homoerratic Radio Show. October 29, 2008.
http://homoerraticradioshow.blogspot.com/2008/10/mickey-
and-mary-carton-and-their.html

Andrew, McNulty. "Mickey Carton." *Find a Grave*. May 26, 2006.
https://www.findagrave.com/memorial/14416281/mickey-carton

Johnson, Ted. "JFK's 'Lost Inaugural Gala': How Sinatra Created
Showbiz's Biggest Political Night." *Variety*. May 27, 2017.
https://variety.com/2017/biz/news/john-f-kennedy-jfk-lost-
inaugural-gala-frank-sinatra-pbs-1202446449/

Purdum, Todd S. "From That Day Forth." *Vanity Fair*. February 2011.
https://archive.vanityfair.com/article/2011/2/from-that-day-forth

Tauber, Gilbert. "Mickey Carton Way." *NYC Streets*. Accessed July
13, 2021. http://www.oldstreets.com/honor.asp?title=Carton

Daw Henson

Henson, Dawson. "The Moonshiner AFS Number 1498A." *The
Lomax Kentucky Recordings*. The Association for Cultural
Equity, Berea College, The Library of Congress, and the
University of Kentucky. Recorded November 10, 1938. Accessed
July 13, 2021. https://lomaxky.omeka.net/items/show/833

"Making the Recordings." *The Lomax Kentucky Recordings, The Lomax
Kentucky Recordings*. The Association for Cultural Equity, Berea
College, The Library of Congress, and the University of Kentucky.
Accessed July 13, 2021. https://lomaxky.omeka.net/lomaxtech

Szwed, John. *Alan Lomax: The Man Who Recorded The World*.
Viking published by the Penguin Group. New York, 2010.

Kenneth Begley

Begley, Kenneth. "The Moonshiner Song. AFS Number 1453B1."
The Lomax Kentucky Recordings. The Association for Cultural
Equity, Berea College, The Library of Congress, and the

University of Kentucky. October 1, 1937. Accessed July 13, 2021. https://lomaxky.omeka.net/items/show/686

Buell Kazee
Chairshotrecords. "Buell Kazee-Rock Island/Old Whisker Bill, The Moonshiner." *Discogs*. Accessed July 13, 2021. https://www.discogs.com/Buell-Kazee-Rock-Island-Old-Whisker-BillMoonshiner/release/7886110
Kazee, Buell. Wikipedia, Wikimedia Foundation Inc., May 16, 2021. https://en.wikipedia.org/wiki/Buell_Kazee
Williams, Pastor Stan. "Buell H. Kazee Part-Time Banjo Picker; Full-Time Servant of Christ." *Kentucky Baptist Heritage*. Newsletter of the Kentucky Baptist Archives Advisory Board. May 4, 2004. http://baptisthistoryhomepage.com/kazee.buell.bio.html

Chapter 8: You May Know Him

I spoke with a manager, two bookers and multiple people at labels but no one had Cat Power's tour dates. Some blamed the inability to access old office hard drives due to the pandemic. Others couldn't find their binders. It was almost as if her tour didn't exist. Luckily, a messageboard had a detailed, and seemingly accurate, tour itinerary which YouTube and other tour accounts online helped to clarify.

Jim Romeo in discussion with the author, May 2021.
Breihan, Tom. "Live: Cat Power's Shitty Night." *The Village Voice*. February 7, 2008. https://www.villagevoice.com/2008/02/07/live-cat-powers-shitty-night/
"cat power @ ISC, Berne Switzerland (1998-11-26) [FULL SHOW]." Music Lover, April 29, 2016. YouTube video, 1:10:25. https://www.youtube.com/watch?v=pqn-7dE27xE

"CAT POWER live Athens, GA 1998." Vaughn Sterling, February 6, 2014. YouTube video, 0:55:36. https://www.youtube.com/watch?v=Jv7UTCGD4hI

German national radio FM-DAT-CDR. "Cat Power @ München, Germany (1998/11/23) [FULL SHOW]." Music Lover, February 5, 2016. YouTube video, 00:48:53. https://www.youtube.com/watch?v=vVi6YMyt-zQ

Mullen, Frank. *Cat Power with Empire State, Echo Lounge, Atlanta*. Ink19. December 23, 1998. https://ink19.com/1999/02/magazine/event-reviews/cat-power-2

"Performance Chronology 1991–2002." odetochan. forumgratuit. April 15, last edited October 22. Accessed July 14, 2021. https://odetochan.forumgratuit.org/t406-performance-chronology-1991-2002

Planet Claire / Aligre 93.1 FM. "Cat Power: Planet Caire Session (1998-11-20)." *Bandcamp*, Planet Claire, November 20, 1998. Streaming audio. https://planetclaire.bandcamp.com/album/cat-power-planet-claire-session-1998-11-20

The Wedge, Canada. "Cat Power - Interview 1999." vacantmoon, April 11, 2012. YouTube video, 0:07:46. https://www.youtube.com/watch?v=94s6O-xddNk

Chapter 9: Colors and the Kids

Ben Ratliff's patience, guidance and thought were beyond helpful during the process of writing this book. His experience as a music writer intimidated but also made me see how a writer can grow.

Ben Ratliff in discussion with author, May 2021.

Baltin, Steve. "Cat Power Gets Some Satisfaction." *Rolling Stone*. March 31, 2000. https://www.rollingstone.com/music/music-news/cat-power-gets-some-satisfaction-184737/

"Catpower: A Fan's Account of 30 Concerts over 13 Years." *Ode to Chan*. August 27. Accessed July 14, 2021. https://odetochan.forumgratuit.org/t261-cat-power-a-fan-s-account-of-30-concerts-over-13-years

Havilla, Rob. "Cat Power Sounds Unchanged Yet Reborn." *The Ringer*. October 6, 2018. https://www.theringer.com/music/2018/10/6/17940794/cat-power-chan-marshall-wanderer-review-interview

Hoby, Hermione. "Cat Power 'I'm Your Worst Nightmare—get Your dancing shoes on'." *The Guardian*. August 18, 2012. https://www.theguardian.com/music/2012/aug/18/cat-power-interview-sun

Pinnock, Tom. "Cat power_Redemption Songs." *Uncut*. September 7, 2012. https://www.uncut.co.uk/features/cat-power-redemption-songs-30365/

Ratliff, Ben. *Every Song Ever: Twenty Ways to Listen in an Age of Musical Plenty*. Farrar, Straus and Giroux Farrar, Straus and Giroux. 2016.

Ratliff, Ben. "Pop Review: Performance Anxiety: Hiding on Stage." *New York Times*. January 5, 1999. https://www.nytimes.com/1999/01/05/arts/pop-review-performance-anxiety-hiding-onstage.html

Smith, Nicky. "All the Things That Truly Make You Feel." *Splice Today*. August 29, 2012. https://www.splicetoday.com/music/all-the-things-that-truly-make-you-feel

van Meter, William. "I'm A Survivor." *New York Magazine*. January 12, 2006. https://nymag.com/nymetro/arts/music/15528/

Chapter 10: Cross Bones Style

When interviewing concertgoers no one could corroborate the date, or the time of the show, but they could remember the overlapping current of emotions forever a part of them and the music.

Ben in discussion with author, May 2021.

Jen in discussion with author, February 2021.

Mark in discussion with author, February 2021.

Matthew in discussion with author, March 2021.

Tracy. E-mail message to author, April 21, 2021.

Rachel, T. Cole. "Cat Power." *Interview*. July 22, 2012. https://www.interviewmagazine.com/music/cat-power

Sarig, Roni. "Cover Story: Cat's meow." *Creative Loafing*. March 12, 2003. https://creativeloafing.com/content-184646-cover-story-cat-s-meow

van Meter, William. "I'm a Survivor." *New York Magazine*. January 12, 2006. https://nymag.com/nymetro/arts/music/15528/

Chapter 11: Peking Saint

The uncanny and the familiar are the biggest comforts and the biggest fears.

Breihan, Tom. "*Moon Pix* Turns 20." *Stereogum*. September 21, 2018. https://www.stereogum.com/2015198/cat-power-moon-pix/reviews/the-anniversary/

Fell, Annie. "Cat Power's 'Moon Pix' Album Is the Greatest." *Riot Fest*. June 26, 2018. https://riotfest.org/2018/06/cat-power-moon-pix-is-the-greatest/

Fricke, David and Sheffield, Rob. *The Year in Recording. MOON Pix Cat power*. Rolling Stone. 12/24/98-01/07/99, Issue 802/803, p160. http://web.a.ebscohost.com/ehost/detail/detail?vid=13&sid=3928e663-c7cf-4c3e-8740-6a68aa965bf7%40sdc-v-sessmgr01&bdata=JkF1dGhUeXBlPWl

wLGNvb2tpZSx1cmwsdWlkJnNpdGU9ZWhvc3QtbGl2ZSSzY
29wZT1zaXRl#AN=1410578&db=aph

Greene, Jayson. "Cat Power; Moon Pix." *Pitchfork*. July 28, 2019.
   https://pitchfork.com/reviews/albums/cat-power-moon-pix/

Hennessy, Kate. "Cat Power on Moon Pix: 'I'm alive today because
   of those songs.' *The Guardian*. May 27, 2018. https://www.
   theguardian.com/music/2018/may/28/cat-power-on-moon-
   pix-im-alive-today-because-of-those-songs

Lagace, Lisa. "Shocking Omissions: Cat Power, 'Moon Pix.'" *NPR*.
   November 6, 2017. https://www.npr.org/2017/
   11/06/561827520/shocking-omissions-cat-power-moon-pix

Saunders, Dudley. *What would the community think*. Rolling Stone.
   11/14/96, Issue 747, p58. https://web.s.ebscohost.com/ehost/
   detail/detail?vid=5&sid=3b9970e7-0110-4cb4-b173-c6ed202
   2479c%40redis&bdata=JkF1dGhUeXBlPWlwLGNvb2tpZSx1
   cmwsdWlkJnNpdGU9ZWhvc3QtbGl2ZSSzY29wZT1zaXRl#
   AN=9612137818&db=f5h

Sobchack, Vivian. "Toward a Phenomenology of Nonfiction Film
   Experience." *Collecting Visible Evidence*, edited by Jane M.
   Gaines and Michael Renov. University of Minnesota Press.
   Minneapolis, 1999.

Wallace, Scott. "Classic Review: Cat Power's Moon Pix." *Sydney
   Scoop*. March 20, 2018. http://sydneyscoop.com/arts-
   entertainment-features/classic-review-cat-powers-moon-pix/

Also Available